PRISONERS

Alexander Solzhenitsyn

Prisoners

A TRAGEDY
TRANSLATED FROM THE RUSSIAN BY
HELEN RAPP AND NANCY THOMAS

THE BODLEY HEAD

LONDON   SYDNEY
TORONTO

Originally published by YMCA Press, Paris, 1981
as *Plenniki*

British Library Cataloguing
in Publication Data
Solzhenitsyn, Aleksandr
Prisoners.
I. Title   II. Plenniki. *English*
891.72'44   PG3488.04
ISBN 0-370-30487-X

World copyright © Alexander Solzhenitsyn 1981
Translation © The Bodley Head Ltd
and Farrar, Straus & Giroux Inc 1983
Printed in Great Britain for
The Bodley Head Ltd
9 Bow Street, London WC2E 7AL
by Redwood Burn Ltd, Trowbridge
Set in Linotron 202 Ehrhardt
by Wyvern Typesetting Ltd, Bristol
First published in Great Britain 1983

DRAMATIS PERSONAE

KLIMOV, Peter, former prisoner of war, Sergeant in the Red Army, now Private in the American Army, 25 years of age

KULYBYSHEV, Kuzma, former prisoner of war, Private in a unit of conscripted prisoners, 40 years of age

BOLOSNIN, Igor, former Lieutenant in the Red Army, now Ensign in the Russian Liberation Army, 30

PRYANCHIKOV, Valentin, former prisoner of war, former officer in the Red Army, 28

PECHKUROV, Ivan, former prisoner of war, Private, 23

YELESHEV, Anatoliy, former prisoner of war, formerly officer in the Red Army, 40

MEDNIKOV, Vasiliy (Vasya), former prisoner of war, 23

VOROTYNTSEV, George, Colonel in the Russian Imperial Army, 69

RUBIN, Leo, Major in the Political Section of the Red Army, 33

KHOLUDENEV, Andrew, Captain in the Red Army, 26

GAI, Paul, Sergeant in the Red Army, 24

TEMIROV, Captain in the Russian Imperial Army, Captain in the Royal Yugoslav Army, about 60

DIVNICH, Eugene, under 40

MOSTOVSHCHIKOV, defector, Professor of physics, over 50

PRISONER with a goatee beard

PRISONER with horn-rimmed spectacles

HALBERAU, Oberleutnant in the Wehrmacht

WRZESNIK, Leon, Second Lieutenant in the Polish Army

DAVYDOV, Major, Quartermaster in the Red Army

FIACENTE, Giovanni, Corporal in the Italian Army

PRISONER with a black eye

SIDOROV

PAKHOMOV

POSVYANTSEVA, Anastasiya, 28–30

POSVYANTSEV, Vsevolod, her husband, an émigré, Subaltern in the Russian Liberation Army, 28

KOLOSOVITOV, Theodore, about 40

NEKLYUCHIMOV, Alexander, Lieutenant in the N.K.G.B., 28

GENERAL, Head of the front-line Department of Counter-Intelligence SMERSH, young and handsome.

RUBLYOV, Prokhor, his deputy, Colonel, about 55

OKHREYANOV, Luka, second deputy, Colonel

KRIVOSHCHAP, President of the military tribunal, Colonel

MORGOSLEPOV, prosecuting Counsel, Lieutenant Colonel

KASHEVAROV, official defence lawyer

KAPUSTIN, Major in the N.K.G.B.

OGNIDA, Major in the N.K.G.B.

KAMCHUZHNAYA, Lydia, Captain in the N.K.G.B.

MYMRA, Captain in the N.K.G.B.

SVERBYOZHNIKOV, Lieutenant in the N.K.G.B., a novice investigator

LVOVA, Sophia, Head of the Medical Unit, Lieutenant Colonel in the Medical Corps

FILIPPOV, Captain in the escort army, front-line soldier

NINEL, typist

1st OPERATIVE

2nd OPERATIVE

GEORGE, General's orderly

1st ASSESSOR of the tribunal

2nd ASSESSOR of the tribunal

KHOLUDENEV'S escort at the trial

Officers, Sergeants, Supervisors, escort soldiers

Prisoners

Waitresses, typists, secretaries

Dramatis personae

The action takes place in one of the Counter-Intelligence centres of SMERSH of the Red Army on 9th July 1945, from one midnight to the next.

(Note to Producers: A shorter version of the play can omit Scenes 6, 8 and ii.)

PUBLISHER'S NOTE

Some parts of this play are in iambic verse
in the original Russian.
The translators' notes are printed on page 147.

Scene 1

A cheerless howling of dogs, resembling that of wolves, can be heard from somewhere. It dies down, as the conversation begins. The scene is the back yard of a prison, badly lit and bounded on three sides by the walls of the three-storey prison building. The only light comes from a wood fire underneath a large cauldron in the middle of the stage. Next to the cauldron a platform has been fixed up with a ladder leading to it. Two people dressed in black, in fur hats, the ear flaps raised and sticking out like horns, are fussing around the cauldron, the elder one climbing up from time to time to stir the contents with a baker's shovel. There are logs around the fire. People sit around the fire on up-turned logs, or lie on the ground. They are Yeleshev and Kholudenev, Vorotyntsev and Pechkurov, Kulybyshev, Klimov and Gai. Halberau is busy twisting a thread. Fiacente is either making or cleaning a cigarette holder. Davydov is lying with his back to everybody. He has spread out some food in little bags and is eating.

Two couples keep walking about: Mostovshchikov and Divnich, and Temirov and Rubin. They walk in arcs or figures-of-eight, either in front or at the back of the stage.

All their heads are shaved and they are almost naked; one is in shorts, another has tied a towel round his midriff, Rubin is wrapped in a sheet. Kholudenev and Davydov wear officers' fur jerkins with nothing underneath. Temirov is in a Caucasian felt cloak. Mostovshchikov wears pince-nez. Vorotyntsev has a little round, grey beard, while Rubin's is long and black.

TEMIROV (*coming out accompanied by Rubin*): I will *not* deny that your knowledge of uniforms is impeccable, but to suggest that the Life Guard Cuirassiers . . .

RUBIN: Yes, they did wear white plumes! (*They go past.*)

MOSTOVSHCHIKOV (*coming out accompanied by Divnich*):
Your kind of Christianity is tough. You bring not peace, but
a sword.

DIVNICH: What do you expect us to do? Do you want us to lie
down like emaciated slaves before a Juggernaut? (*They go
past.*)

KLIMOV: We'll never understand those Americans. I suppose
we're too slow-witted. There's an issue of tinned veal, nice
and pink. There are no holes in the tins, just a dent. Never
mind, they throw them out as damaged. Or else huge boxes
full of ship's biscuits. If the packing is slightly squashed, out
they go into a ditch. (*He laughs.*)

HALBERAU (*singing as he works*):
> Und warst du krank, sie pflegte dich,
> Den sie mit tiefen Schmerz geboren.
> Und gaben alle dich schon auf –
> Die Mutter gab dich nicht verloren.

PECHKUROV: I would have joined the Russian Liberation
Army, or worked for the Police. Instead, just think, four
years in a prison camp. I was never put in charge, nobody
gave me a stick to wield. I got no privileges at someone else's
expense. I just walked up and down, emptying slop pails. If
only we'd been liberated by the Americans! But, no! It had to
be our lot!

VOROTYNTSEV: *Our* lot, Ivan? What's *ours* about them? The
sound of their names? A Russian cast of face? But after all
the executions, camps, collectivisation, that spongeful of
vinegar – in what way are they *ours*?

RUBIN (*coming out accompanied by Temirov*): Yes, I *am* a Communist, an orthodox one what's more, and whatever my
personal fate . . . (*They go past.*)

GAI (*his wounded right arm in a sling*): So our Soviet General
shouts: 'Soldiers, come back!' And the American General
says: 'What for?' 'Excuse me,' says our General, 'you are
guests here. Our custom is for simple soldiers to eat at the
same table as the Generals!'

KLIMOV: Well said!!

GAI: So, naturally, they rush forward for the grub.

KLIMOV: That was a lesson in democracy, no two ways about it.

(*Temirov and Rubin are by-passing Davydov, who is chewing. Davydov catches hold of Rubin's sheet.*)

DAVYDOV: Comrade Rubin. Come and sit down, have some of this simple food my friends sent me ... There's no one I can talk to. The only true Soviets in this prison are you and me.

RUBIN: I think, Comrade Davydov, I ought not to be in a hurry about making friends just now. (*He goes past.*)

YELESHEV (*to Kholudenev*): My young friend, even though my head is crowned with silver hair – (*he lifts his hand to his hair*) Oh, I forgot, it's shaved ... But I am bound to say that I devoted my entire life to women and I have no regrets.

DIVNICH (*coming out with Mostovshchikov*): Yes, I grow silent before the star-studded vault of the night sky, and when I see the hues of dawn or of sunset, I grow silent at the sight of the repentant tears of a fellow human being. I love the frailty of human flesh. Our Lord decreed that we should love sinners – but when people are virtuous ... (*They go past.*)

RUBIN (*to Temirov*): Do you know, they're as stubborn as mules, the way they keep quoting their book of rules. I can't stand it sometimes and answer back with a barbed retort. I'm a thorn in the flesh of the political section. And yet, what do they do themselves? They spend their time getting parcels together to send to their wives. They're looters, scroungers. Call them political workers! But who'm I saying this to? You're delighted! You laugh! (*They go past.*)

DAVYDOV (*having tied up his little bags, speaking to Fiacente over his shoulder*): Giovanni, have a rusk.

(*Fiacente takes it rapidly and bows.*)

DAVYDOV (*after some thought*): Here! There's a bit left to go with your rusk – you can scrape off the sides and the bottom with your finger.

(*He hands over a small jar, which Fiacente takes with one hand, while pressing his other hand to his heart. He bows.*)

GAI: He used to be the Commander of our regiment. He was sensible, firm, self-controlled. He used to say: 'You can see for yourself how you spent your war, who we shed our blood for.' When will we learn? . . . It's a sad admission, but it seems, wherever you're best off, that's where you belong. He was good at English. He pushed the four of us into a jeep – and onto the bridge!

RUBIN (*coming out with Temirov*): I'm an ass to have started a conversation with you!

TEMIROV: You're a destroyer of human hopes. Shame on you. Shame!

RUBIN: And you're a sad remnant of Kolchak's army. An Imperial hanger-on!

TEMIROV: But never a Communist, no, never a stinking Communist!

RUBIN: Yes, prisons are a good thing if it's people like you who're in them.

TEMIROV: At least I'm among strangers, while you are with your own kind. (*They abruptly part company.*)

GAI: I jumped off and hit out with the butt of my gun and suddenly I saw the jeep. Hullo there! But they arrested me then.

PECHKUROV (*to Vorotyntsev*): The doors are shut, the keys are turned, you're surrounded by wolves in the night. We'll shoot you, we'll hang you . . . Well, I haven't got nine lives. You can write any damn thing you like in your report. I'll sign it without reading it, just leave me alone.

VOROTYNTSEV: But that's just it. That's the fatal mistake. Our weak, tattered, oppressed willpower is weighed down by this enormity, by their entire apparatus. Its sharp end is pointed right at us. During these unbearable but numbered nights, Ivan, we must, we must cling on by our fingertips. We must resist this uncontrolled gallop, this snorting, this foaming at the mouth if we're to keep some self respect.

DIVNICH (*coming out with Mostovshchikov*): I managed to resist the Gestapo with the help of God's strong hand, and with God's mercy I'll survive the G.P.U. (*They go past.*)

RUBIN (*putting his arms around Yeleshev and Kholudenev, who are sitting down*): Well, sons of Russia! Don't let's complain about our present troubles. After all, we've always had an Eastern despotism . . . Everything that seems so hard on our little selves will pass. In the balance of History we don't count for much . . .

GAI: The anti-aircraft guns were out of ammunition. There I was on a bridge over the river and I managed to bring down a couple of Messerschmitts, fighting like a maniac for that bunch of . . . (*He wails, holding his head.*)

KULYBYSHEV: Never mind, son, it's no use crying over spilt milk. You can't make omelettes without breaking eggs. The surf is full of sand before the sea calms down. And your brain is just as addled.

RUBIN (*now with Divnich*): Yes, I accept Christianity. Having once adhered to a principle, I try to treasure it. But if that principle turns out to be wrong, I find solace only in Christianity. From Graeco-Roman times to the heights of German genius there's been no better teaching, and I am ready to follow the path of the Son of Man. I would drink from the cup of Gethsemane! But I have in mind the teachings of Christ, not the dogmas of the Church . . . (*They go past.*)

MOSTOVSHCHIKOV: Now, the King of Norway is a darling. He wanders about Oslo, having nothing better to do; he will drink a mug of beer in a pub with his subjects, will invite some learned foreigner to visit him, he never loses his temper, never gets ruffled, while his wife, the Queen, goes to market with her maid.

VOROTYNTSEV (*to Pechkurov*): We clutch at life with convulsive intensity   that's how we get caught. We want to go on living at any, *any* price. We accept all the degrading conditions, and this way we save – not ourselves – we save the persecutor. But he who doesn't value his life is unconquerable, untouchable. There are such people! And if you become one of them, then it's not you but your persecutor who'll tremble!

YELESHEV (*to Kholudenev*): I devoted all my talents, all my emotions to them! My every action was dedicated to them. As an architect, I built houses for them, I shone in society, I was the life and soul of the party – all for their sake!

KHOLUDENEV: Listening to this makes me furious! I wasted my youth poring over books! But now I'm so randy I could howl like a wolf – after any woman. (*Fiacente is humming some passionate Italian song.*) Now, I'll be condemned to ten years . . . in some distant Arctic darkness . . . while all I want to do is run after female footprints in the sand like some wretched little dog.

(*Kholudenev has lowered his head. Rubin is now pestering Kulybyshev.*)

RUBIN: Yes, I did come across collective farms which were prosperous; they had cows, sheeps, pigs, goats . . .

Pryanchikov and the 1st Supervisor[1] enter quickly from the back of the stage and walk past the cauldron. The Supervisor wears a soiled white overall on top of his uniform. The spectator cannot at first discern what is wrong with Pryanchikov's extremely elegant suit and his awkward movements – but all the buttons of his clothes have been cut off, and are more or less held together by string. Pryanchikov's movements are rapid but constrained, as if he is afraid of dropping something.

PRYANCHIKOV (*still walking*): Why is it, Comrade, that you address both the military and civilians in exactly the same way: 'Get going, get going!' Eh, Comrade?

1ST SUPERVISOR: Comrade my foot! Wolf, more like! Into the cauldron with those rags.

PRYANCHIKOV (*having removed a soft felt hat, lets his thick brown hair fall around his head. He lifts his right arm in a quick salute*): Heil Hitler, gentlemen! (*Thrusting his right arm for-*

ward): Long live Comrade Stalin! (*Waving lightly to Fiacente*):
Viva Mussolini! (*Waving both arms*): Živeo Mihailović! May I
introduce myself? I'm Valentin Pryanchikov. I'm agitating
against our return to the U.S.S.R. (*Yeleshev sidles up to him
and whispers something into his ear. Pryanchikov loudly*): I've
been warned, I know that there are stooges among us from
Counter Intelligence. But being an honest man, I do not
propose to hide – (*behind his back the Supervisor is blowing into
the head-shaving razor. The conversations and movements have
stopped. Pryanchikov is the centre of attention*) – that I am in
close contact with world bourgeoisie, and almost out of
touch with the world proletariat. My turnover capital is three
hundred thousand francs. I own a house, a car and a wife – in
Brussels. (*Sits down on a log.*)

IST SUPERVISOR: How about lice? Got any?

PRYANCHIKOV: What did you say?

IST SUPERVISOR: Lice.

PRYANCHIKOV (*bursts out laughing, loses his balance and would
have fallen off the log, if he had not supported himself with one
hand on the ground*): Ha-ha-ha! I haven't laughed like that for
a long time. Where would I get them from, you cannibals,
you blockheads? I've arrived from Europe, not Moscow!

IST SUPERVISOR: Didn't I tell you to take everything off and
throw it into the cauldron?

WORKMAN (*from above the cauldron*): Comrade Supervisor!
There's hardly any water left.

IST SUPERVISOR: All right. You needn't do it.

PRYANCHIKOV: Grand merci! I'm glad. In this country of
ours we enjoy such simple pleasures. Oh yes. I quite forgot,
gentlemen, to ask you just one question. Has the level of
production not increased? Dear me! Things are still in a bad
way? I judge by the fact that the Military have cut off all my
buttons! I can't keep my trousers up.

KLIMOV: Were they made of metal?

PRYANCHIKOV: Certainly not. Ivory

KLIMOV: Ever so chic, then?

PRYANCHIKOV: Naturally. Cream-coloured.

KLIMOV: That means, they took them for their *parcels*. Never you mind, friend. Everybody's buttons get cut off.

PRYANCHIKOV: But what am I to do?

KLIMOV: We'll make you some out of bread.

PRYANCHIKOV (*looking around for the first time*): But, what on earth is going on here?

TEMIROV: Bath time.

PRYANCHIKOV: Under the open sky? How peculiar!

KHOLUDENEV: What is peculiar?

PRYANCHIKOV: Where's the water, the shower, the bath-tub?

YELESHEV: The shower and the bath-tub are only half the trouble.

PECHKUROV: The trouble is . . .

KLIMOV and KULYBYSHEV (*together*): There is no water!
Pryanchikov, quite stunned, stops fidgeting and sits down on a log. At this point the Supervisor has finished cleaning the razor and comes up from behind to start shaving his head.

PRYANCHIKOV: Then why did they bring us out here?

KHOLUDENEV: For delousing. According to schedule.

PRYANCHIKOV (*putting his hand on the top of his head*): Hey, who's there? (*Jumps up, runs away and touches the shaven spot.*)

1ST SUPERVISOR: What's biting you? Do you want to be hand-cuffed? Locked up?

PRYANCHIKOV: Wait, I've been locked up – in a kind of coffin. Put in there, still alive. (*Touching his bald patch.*) What have you done? I shall complain!

1ST SUPERVISOR: To hell with you! Will you sit still, you fidget.

PRYANCHIKOV: What about the Atlantic Charter? You're transgressing it! . . . Aren't you? (*His last question is directed at Yeleshev.*)

YELESHEV (*in a whisper*): Give in, old chap! Everybody's been shaved. Just look around . . .
Pryanchikov turns around, examining everybody's heads. His

cockiness has vanished. He sits down and the shaving begins.
Rubin sits down in front of Pryanchikov on a pile of logs.

RUBIN: So there you are, Comrade. Even though your head is
not quite shaved yet, behind these walls we get to know one
another quite quickly, so I can inform you that from now on
you are a paid-up member of cell one hundred and twenty-
five, which maintains well tried and age-old prison traditions. One of those traditions, I must tell you, is that we
interview the newcomer. Get ready. Are you a citizen of the
U.S.S.R.?

PRYANCHIKOV: Alas . . .

RUBIN: Right. We'll not enquire about your grandmother and
grandfather, just yet. Your profession?

PRYANCHIKOV: Engineer.

RUBIN: And your age?

PRYANCHIKOV: Twenty-eight.

RUBIN: You don't look it.

PRYANCHIKOV: Merci.

RUBIN: Been a member of the Party?

PRYANCHIKOV: Heaven forbid!

RUBIN: But you belonged to the All-Union Leninist Communist Youth League.

PRYANCHIKOV: I was . . .

RUBIN: How do you mean?

PRYANCHIKOV: I mean, I was stupid enough to . . .

RUBIN: Don't let's make value judgements. That's an ideological division between us. When you left University, were
you married?

PRYANCHIKOV: Oh, my Madeleine!

RUBIN: Judging by her name, you're giving me some extra
information. Then – the War?

PRYANCHIKOV: Yes, the War.

RUBIN: And a prisoner of war?

PRYANCHIKOV: And a prisoner after a bit.

RUBIN: Which camp?

PRYANCHIKOV: In Rhine-Westphalia.

RUBIN: What kind of labour?

PRYANCHIKOV: Ore mines. Most unpleasant, I might add.

RUBIN: And you've served your term?

PRYANCHIKOV: We escaped.

RUBIN: Where to, it would be interesting to know?

PRYANCHIKOV: To Belgium. To the Ardennes. Gentlemen, this is fascinating. They have a thing there called the . . . the Resistance. You should see those partisans! Rosy-cheeked boys, old egg-heads, all join the underground, north, south, east and west. They hide where they can't be found and – do they resist! They refuse to work in factories, or join the army . . . While the whole of Europe is in a monstrous uproar, we've taken refuge among trees, above us – branches and birds. And Belgian girls bring us food. What girls! . . .

RUBIN: Madeleine?

PRYANCHIKOV: I can't deny it. The invasion and all that . . .

RUBIN: So you grew rich, on your dowry?

PRYANCHIKOV: Yes. But in ten months I trebled it!

Davydov, clearing his throat loudly, approaches and listens with great attention. The shaving has finished. The 1st Supervisor leaves.

RUBIN: Don't try and convince us that the economic theories of Adam Smith or David Ricardo . . .

PRYANCHIKOV: Excuse me! And don't make such faces. I know all about it. I know all about Marx-Engels, Lapidus-Ostrovityanov. The point is that over there you are not oppressed, pushed or pulled around! In one year over there I became a businessman. I'm not joking. Some managed to earn millions. We, the Soviet people, don't know our own talents. Over there, let's face it, there is no G.P.U. or finance inspectors! If you're the proud possessor of *une tête* and an extra franc . . .

DAVYDOV: One can do business? . . .

PRYANCHIKOV: Yes, *argent*! (*He laughs.*) It's funny, gentlemen. We're so used to a leaden weight on our backs, to being pushed down, to outside pressure, that when we find ourselves in the West we're like earthlings on the moon, leaping rather than walking. We're bounced into success.

RUBIN: What rubbish you talk, my friend! You argue like a shopkeeper! Somebody must pay the increased cost . . .

DIVNICH (*coming forward and gently taking Rubin by his shoulders*): Comrade Rubin, you mustn't presume on the rights of an interviewer. (*To Pryanchikov*): If your arguments are so sound, what did you come back for?

PRYANCHIKOV: Who, me? I got stolen.

A VOICE: How do you mean, stolen?

PRYANCHIKOV: Just like that, in broad daylight. In Brussels.

VOICES: Where? Whom? When? Not possible!

PRYANCHIKOV: Gentlemen, what do you take me for? Do you think I'm subnormal or something – to come back of my own free will?

KULYBYSHEV: There are some such . . .

YELESHEV: Who spent the whole war in the West . . .

PECHKUROV: Who suffered everything . . .

KLIMOV: Who went through fire . . .

PRYANCHIKOV: And – who returned?

KLIMOV: And who returned.

PRYANCHIKOV: They must be mad!

VOROTYNTSEV: It's difficult to say. What's more normal – to have complete faith, or to reject faith altogether?

PRYANCHIKOV: Anyway, the war came to an end. And *Comrades* arrived in their hundreds, elegantly dressed in civvies and rosettes with gold inscriptions. (*Speaking rapidly.*) Wherever there's an Ambassador and an Embassy, in they go through every crevice, dozens of plenipotentiaries, two hundred and twenty attachés, a staff of three hundred and forty to round up Russian 'Ivans'. Well, what could they do – it's awkward to refuse an allied nation! The representatives of the Repatriation scheme say: 'Your mothers or your sisters await you in devastated towns. And even if you fought against your brother Ivan, even if you spilt the blood of innocent babes, gun in hand, your country will forgive. Your country calls you back!' It worked, as I observed. They went like lambs . . .

MOSTOVSHCHIKOV How feckless, how trusting is your average Russian.

PRYANCHIKOV: I did what I could. Whoever I met, I'd try and talk them out of it, beg them to avoid it like the plague. 'Are you short of cash? – Here, let me lend you some.' 'Can't find any work? – Here, I'll give you a reference.' Why did I care? I was sorry for my countrymen. And yet, I was betrayed. And who did it? The closest friend I escaped from the camp with . . .

KHOLUDENEV (*to Mostovshchikov*): That's typical of us, the Soviets . . .

PRYANCHIKOV: We met. 'Need any help?' I write a cheque for him . . . 'No, no, no need,' he says; 'I've decided to return.' 'Do you remember what it was like on the Rhine? The way it was with the Partisans? . . . All right. Shall we have a farewell dinner?' I book at the most fashionable restaurant. Anybody been to Brussels? It was there that this Judas pointed me out. I pay my bill, I leave, and no sooner do the swing doors close behind me than I'm hit on the head – and how! Right across the pavement and into a car, head first!

VOICES: Passers-by? Police?

PRYANCHIKOV: I can't remember. It only took a second, it was like lightning! Well, there I am in the Embassy, recovering, but – I'm not going to give in, I'm going to defend myself in Belgium . . .

DAVYDOV: But who . . . who got your money?

PRYANCHIKOV: I was sort of gagged, everything went through the diplomatic bag, without inspection, to the frontier, through to Amsterdam . . .

A VOICE: But there?

PRYANCHIKOV: And from there to the airport. From London it was Soviet pilots who flew to Berlin. They'd been on a good-will mission, or a friendly mission. The Devil alone

can sort that out. Those Dutch cheeseheads never opened my bags – and off into a 'plane. We landed in the Soviet zone. I hadn't understood, even then, but I did when two soldiers took charge of me. They were eating soup out of a mess tin, sitting astride a couple of logs. They offered me a spoon: 'Sit down, friend, the soup is good.' I tried it . . . (*He makes a gesture of throwing the spoon away, wailing.*) Oh mother Russia! Oh this country of ours!
They all droop. Silence.

DIVNICH: This country of ours, built of straw, evil-smelling, barbarous, lawless and despairing . . .

RUBIN: With slavery in our bones, slavery through to the marrow . . .

DIVNICH: Oh my motherland, you look so menacing in the dark before dawn, when the bright light of the war has grown dim. To look at you from the border, you appear half dead, speechless, smothered by the blind, unfeeling, blunt will of 'Prince' Dzhugashvili . . .[2]

GAI: If they let us in from here, from Europe, we'll turn Stalin into dust and smoke!

RUBIN: You're mad! You're blind. Do you think you can turn the wheel of history back again . . . ?

KHOLUDENEV: No, we'll just wait for the Security Services to give us thirty-five years!

RUBIN: But, friends, we're not the first to go back from a tidy Europe into an unwashed Russia. A hundred years ago other regiments felt nauseated at the thought. But then, on the impoverished and exhausted soil a wonderful flowering took place. It produced the Muravievs, the Trubetskoys, the Pestels.[3] Now it's our turn, the turn of our generation. They did, though, crown their rebellion by reaching the Senate Square, while we're arrested on the Asian border and are prisoners of SMERSH.

VOROTYNTSEV: No, forgive me, your analogy is all wrong. If we *are* to have a rebellion, God willing, it won't be launched with the aristocratic bubbling of champagne and oysters on a

silver salver, nor will it be like those borrowed dreams from
distant days and far away places. It'll be done by thick-set
people who will have had enough of their prison soup.

YELESHEV: Of course, your idea that we're the latter-day
Decembrists is beautiful, but why be so gloomy? There's
bound to be an amnesty.

PRYANCHIKOV (*animated*): Is an amnesty expected?

YELESHEV: But of course, well before we reach Siberia.

PRYANCHIKOV: And soon?

YELESHEV: Any minute now; two or three days.

PRYANCHIKOV: Does that mean they'll let us go?

KHOLUDENEV: Yes, yes, to our wives and children.

PRYANCHIKOV (*to Kholudenev*): How soon?

KHOLUDENEV: After three or four five-year plans.

YELESHEV: Comrade Kholudenev, you can laugh. But the
investigator was quite specific.

DAVYDOV (*approaching*): He told me that too.

KLIMOV: Don't butt in!

DAVYDOV: Why ever not?

KLIMOV (*fists clenched*): Because didn't you say you had deal-
ings with those Nazi swine . . . ?

TEMIROV (*stepping between them*): You'll be forgiven – you're
just a thief. Never mind that you stole two hundred thousand
– you remain socially close to the Soviet ruling class.

WORKMAN (*from above*): Hey, you! It's ready. Come and get
it!

*He starts throwing out the steaming clothes using the baker's
shovel. There is a general rapid movement as they sort out their
possessions. Chaos.*

RUBIN: They've burnt my shirt, the buggers!

YELESHEV: Oh dear!

*General hubbub and movement. Fiacente, who is still undressed,
has brought Davydov's things and is fussing around him. Pryanchikov, the only one to have remained dressed, observes the scene.*

RUBIN: Anyone got some military trousers?

VOICES: Quiet! Don't shout!

[24]

RUBIN: German ones, torn.

SOMEONE: How about these?

RUBIN: The very things.

He passes them to the Oberleutnant, since they are his. The hubbub increases.

HALBERAU (*to Rubin*): Danke sehr, danke sehr!

A VOICE: How did they make it so dirty, the pigs?

PRYANCHIKOV: I would like to know what would have happened to someone in a dinner jacket.

KHOLUDENEV: What about a dinner jacket?

KLIMOV: What do you mean, what about it? Into the cauldron!

PRYANCHIKOV: Unthinkable!

KLIMOV: Do you know what is unthinkable? Getting your *thing* into a bottle. Everything else is thinkable, my friend . . .

1st and 2nd Supervisors enter.

1ST SUPERVISOR: Line up in twos! Hands behind your backs!

The prisoners line up in a column, two by two, some still getting dressed as they walk. Rubin comes up with a complaint.

RUBIN: Citizen chief, they've burned a hole in my shirt!

1ST SUPERVISOR: You can get it darned in your cell. Ma-arch!

RUBIN (*persisting*): I shall make a complaint! Who's in charge, who's responsible?

2ND SUPERVISOR (*pushing him into line*): March, you in front!

The column disappears into the depths of the yard.

Scene 2

A small cell. There are no bunks, the floor is covered with straw and the prisoners are asleep on the straw, their heads to the wall, their feet stretched into the centre. There is a door with a food hatch and a peep-hole. Next to the door, a wooden barrel slop bucket without a cover. The single window opening is newly bricked up almost to the top; the bricks are unplastered and the opening at the top is tiny and barred. The light in the cell is dim, but it grows perceptibly lighter during the scene.

Divnich is saying his prayers beneath the window. Vorotyntsev and Kholudenev are talking, lying down. Kulybyshev and Wrzesnik are by the door listening to discover what is happening in the corridor. Pryanchikov, being the last arrival, is asleep by the slop bucket. He is recognisable by his hat, which covers his entire head. Klimov's head is towards us. He is close to the audience. He is awake and leaning on his elbows, he sings quietly in a strong, clear voice.

KLIMOV: Where are you, where are you?
    Tell me where you are.
    Why did this war
    Send you quite so far?

    You've been going round and round
    These many wartime years,
    Tell me what encouragements,
    What medals have you found?

The door opens with a clang and in comes a new prisoner, with a black eye, an enormous bruise on his cheekbone. The door shuts with an equally loud clang. All those asleep shudder, without waking up. The newcomer's arms are behind his back, but on finding himself in the cell, he releases them. Klimov, as if hitting himself on the cheekbone:

KLIMOV: The investigator?

PRISONER WITH A BLACK EYE: I value my teeth a great deal, so, whether I had or not, I signed I'd been here, I'd been there . . . (*He squeezes himself among the sleepers and lies down.*)

KLIMOV (*singing*):

> Are you dealing with the mines,
> Do you drive the tanks?
> Are you a pilot, rocket-launcher,
> Do you hide the partisans?
>
> Are you down with typhoid fever?
> Do you live abroad?
> Are you dead, or coming
> Back to Russia with your sword?
> Or can it be they'll lock you up
> In your country as a spy?

WRZESNIK: Take me as an example. The best thing to do is to learn foreign languages. We're ruined for lack of them. I could have been a spy in Great Britain. Instead, I had to do it in the cursed U.S.S.R. No English. How-do-you-do? If-you-please . . . What, you refuse to be locked up in the Tower? Then go to the Bolsheviks and eat their prison soup! Go and build Communism. Where are we? In prison? Rotten straw, mother-fuckers! Now, in Poland, a prison is quite different: you get two sheets, a proper bed, books, a bed-side table. Exercise. You get meat for dinner. White rolls for breakfast!

KLIMOV: What were you in for?

WRZESNIK: I used to be a Communist, more fool me. Once you find yourself here, you see things more clearly . . .

Divnich continues his fervent praying. Klimov is doing a hand stand. He wears nothing but his trunks. His body is beautifully developed.

[27]

KLIMOV (*upside down*): And then?

WRZESNIK: And then, you can go and seek your rights! At first, the Comrades gave us land; then they turned on the heat. I had to serve in the Red Army. Then, suddenly, an order from the Political Section. *Poland still lives* – but whether you're a Catholic, holy Mother of God, or a Party member, Leo Wrzesnik, you're now a Second Lieutenant in the Polish Army.

KLIMOV (*lying down in his previous position, singing*):

> Your wife comes into the garden, all in vain.
> Where are you, where are you?
> Tell me where you are.
> Why did this war
> Send you quite so far?

(*He lowers his head and is quiet.*)

VOROTYNTSEV (*to Kholudenev*): There was no mercy at the altar on which we laid our heads. We didn't recognise each other in our own country. People got greedy, angry and hard, as if everyone had gone off his head. As if they'd given themselves up to the Devil. It wasn't the mistakes of the Generals; it wasn't our principles that were wrong – nothing could have altered the whirling course of events. They just happened, spiralled and rushed on . . . I had the misfortune of taking part in the Russian retreat from Mukden, Naidenburg and from Oryol to Rostov. It was an irresistible retreat. But I was never so bitter as during our departure from the Crimea. I was standing there in a motley, hysterical crowd, some weeping over their losses, some hoping for sustenance. And I said to myself: 'This is "us", always "us", but what about them, those others? Those who lord it over us, in Moscow, who fail to see from their commanding heights?' And I thought, it could just be that I've never known the real Russia, that I've never loved her. But then – surely not Lenin, surely not Trotsky? Perhaps our complaints, our moans are a self-indulgence? After all, we have given *Russia* away as if she were a tiny County of Mecklen-

[28]

burg. Can it be that by promising government by the people, we misjudged the true sources of renewal? . . . As I stood on the ship, the lighthouse of Kherson glimmered once and disappeared in the darkness. O my country, would I ever see you again? And how, and when, and where? . . .

KHOLUDENEV: Now you've seen it.

VOROTYNTSEV: I never thought that I would have to live for so long so far away. The times, the people have changed in the meantime. We did think, however, that we would have the possibility – before we died – of liberating Russia. But – no. Twenty-five years have passed, and still no! And now again, no. How much longer? And again, our allies. They let us down, they give no support. And so our soldiers are in the hands of the Red Army. And it's my fate to end up here, sitting on this rotten straw, eating your undercooked gruel, seeing what you've all become, what you've grown up into, what you have learned. I'm grateful to my Creator that the Bolsheviks are dead long before any of us.

KHOLUDENEV: It was Marx and Lenin who swallowed up large chunks of our youth. Even before we fought in the war, before we'd seen Europe, seen the rays of the sun through these rusty bars – we were, and would have remained, the sheep-like defenders of our country. Did we know who we were, what we were, why they filled our books with trunk-fulls of emptiness?

Divnich has moved over to the door and is talking to Kulybyshev, who is sitting down on the straw.

DIVNICH (*in a prophetic voice*):
It won't be long before the pious people
Will open their churches in a cloud of incense,
Before Russia will ring with church bells
And monasteries will be full again.

Oh my unhappy people, keep your hope,
God's grace will shine over you.
Having astounded the world with your crimes

[29]

You will astound it with your penitence.

People will make new paths to the neglected and reviled sanctuaries,

They will follow their priests, ikons and banners in great multitudes.

KULYBYSHEV (*picking his nose*): Yes. All that's quite true, only I must tell you, I was one of those who closed the churches down. (*Divnich staggers back in surprise.*) I joined the twenty-five thousand. Don't worry – the Party, the Government, Comrade Stalin personally will do the thinking, they said, you just close down this church and turn it into a grain-collecting centre. But, say I, all the women will rebel. Ignorance, they said, what do we care! And I must say, almost the entire village was against it, while we, the activists, signed petitions in their stead, ten times over.

DIVNICH: You too?

KULYBYSHEV: What was I to do? Do you think they could not manage without me? The lambs join the rams.

KHOLUDENEV: How come we managed to grow up without being aware of the presence of the Lubianka, that we were carefree and rosy-cheeked? It's ironic that you fought on the side of Franco, while I dreamed of joining the Republicans.

VOROTYNTSEV: I tasted victory only once there! It was a good battle towards the liberation of Moscow and Oryol that we fought in Madrid and Toledo! We killed at least a couple of hundred.

A key jangles loudly in the lock. Mednikov, pale and shaky, enters and, as if blind, tumbles towards his place. All those who are asleep shudder, as they did the first time, lift their heads and put them down again.

KHOLUDENEV: How was it, Vasiliy?

MEDNIKOV: Six days and nights, dear friends. God, I need some sleep!

DIVNICH: Well then, tell me, old man, do you believe in God?

KULYBYSHEV: What?

DIVNICH: In God, do you believe in God?

KULYBYSHEV: Who, me?

DIVNICH: Yes, you.

KULYBYSHEV: In God?

DIVNICH: In Our Lord, in Our Saviour?

KULYBYSHEV: If you're silent – you're in trouble. If you speak – trouble again. What am I to say? Maybe yes. Maybe no ... Life is full of snares. Suppose you get stomach cramps, you roll on the floor with pain – then you pray to all the saints. But when all is going smoothly, you don't even bother to glance at those old women's ikons. Here, now, we're all traitors to our country. Cut down the raspberries – mow down the blackcurrants. But that's not what I got arrested for. I got arrested for infringing the regulations. I issued extra bread to the collective farm women. Without it, they would have died before the spring. I wasn't doing it for my own good – I had enough food at home. But this thing is choking me, I've had it up to here. This thing, I don't know what to call it – the *thing.*

It seems he is lost in thought, or dozing. Vorotyntsev and Kho-ludenev are also asleep. There is some music, which sounds like a prison waking up. People move about heavily in their places, struggling between sleep and wakefulness. They make remarks, as if in a delirium and drop their heads once again.

YELESHEV: What's happening? Am I asleep or am I dreaming? It was such a lovely dream. It went too soon ... I dreamt again of the golden head of Elsa Kroneberg! My God! To wake up in a prison is terrible. What an oppressive moment. I've been fighting it all night.

ANOTHER VOICE: I have no will to live ...

A THIRD VOICE: Or strength to move ...

A FOURTH VOICE: What is the meaning of the day to come? ...

SOMEONE ELSE: Barely a flicker of light through the bars ...

A loud turning of the key in the lock. Everybody shudders; they lift their heads all together. The door does not open and their heads fall back again.

ANOTHER VOICE: That key turning is like a dagger in your heart.

KHOLUDENEV: My life's been so short. Has it been lived – or not lived at all? Has it been lent to my country in the heat of the moment like a couple of golden sovereigns? . . .

A VOICE: And the only change you get is a worn penny.

ANOTHER: The sun will rise today, but not for us.

PECHKUROV: A German prison – and now a Soviet one . . .

ANOTHER VOICE: During the day you obediently lug your chains.

ANOTHER: You stare dumbly at the bars, at the lock.

ANOTHER: For a prisoner kindly night is a short and cruel gift.

ANOTHER: During the day one gets used to things, as if that's what it should be like. But first thing in the morning this enormous stone structure crushes the breath out of you.

OTHER VOICES: Ten Years! Easily said!

Count on your fingers! . . .

No wife! . . . No mother! . . . No daughter! . . . No home! . . .

Never see it again! . . .

Never to return! . . .

And unable to lift your head from the straw! . . .

And unable to open your eyelids . . .

They are all asleep again. The last bars of the dying melody are interrupted by the grating of keys and the door opening.

4TH SUPERVISOR (*shouting*): To the bog! At the double!

TEMIROV (*being the first to rise*): To the bog! Come on, *parachutists!*

With the exception of Mednikov, all rise, or jump up. General chaos. Wrzesnik tries to be the first through the door.

4TH SUPERVISOR (*to Wrzesnik*): Sto-op! Don't push. You with the slop bucket, go through!

KHOLUDENEV (*holding one handle of the bucket*): Leo.

VOICES: Who are you carrying it with?

With Leo.

RUBIN (*gathering things quickly, keeps forgetting some things. His*

[32]

towel hangs from his neck, gets tangled in his beard, gets in the way): Is it my turn? Can't be. (*He quickly gets hold of the second handle.*)

VOICES: Don't spill it! Don't spill it! . . . Careful!

Rubin and Kholudenev carry the bucket out. The others follow. We can see everybody putting their arms behind their backs and forming into pairs.

KLIMOV (*standing over Mednikov*): Vasiliy! Do get up, old man. That rat will have you on your feet whether you like it or not.

4TH SUPERVISOR (*beyond the door*): Form up in twos. Hands behind your backs.

KLIMOV: Vasiliy!

MEDNIKOV: M-m-m . . .

4TH SUPERVISOR (*running in*): Who else is here? Up you get! (*He kicks the soles of Mednikov's feet with the toe of his boot.*)

MEDNIKOV: I don't need the bog. Let me sleep.

4TH SUPERVISOR: Wha-at? Quoting regulations at me?

MEDNIKOV: Interrogations by night, interrogations by day . . .

4TH SUPERVISOR: Order must be kept!

Everybody is gone.

March!

The column leaves. Enter the 5th Supervisor.

O.K. I do this side. You do the other. (*He indicates the two sides of the cell and the two rows of straw.*)

5TH SUPERVISOR: Do you know, Valeriy, these searches – I may be a fool – they cut me to the quick.

4TH SUPERVISOR: 'Searches' my foot. They're the 'turnovers' here! Forget what happened in the Army. Prisons have their own laws. The Lieutenant said – even if you find nothing, rake it about a bit.

They begin to stir up the straw, throw the belongings about. Having found nothing, they leave. The prisoners return.

VOICES: They've been at the straw again!

Another search! Up theirs!

The buggers!

Everything's been thrown about!

Can't get used to it. God, they make me furious!

They tidy the straw, look for their belongings, spread them out.
Klimov stands motionless in the middle of the cell, arms folded.

KLIMOV: Never mind, brothers, we'll survive. We'll see Stalin hanged yet! He will be tried himself one day!

KULYBYSHEV: You can wait for that, friend, till kingdom come. Mice might drown a cat, but only once it's dead.

Fiacente comes up to Davydov.

DAVYDOV: Bed made up?

FIACENTE: Oh yes, Signor.

DAVYDOV: Now let's see to the sewing. You must learn Russian, you know. You won't be able to manage without it. (*They discuss the making of slippers.*)

YELESHEV (*to Kholudenev*): I bet you never had to lie next to such a filthy wall.

KHOLUDENEV: Go to hell.

YELESHEV: That's rude and silly. You're not a European. You haven't learnt to compromise.

KHOLUDENEV: That's quite an idea – that Europe and compromise are the same. (*He moves a bit and makes room.*)

PECHKUROV (*to Kulybyshev*): I wonder what my dream means. It was about a church.

KULYBYSHEV: That there will be some change in our lives. Those who are free will go to prison. We shall be freed. It's a good thing to dream in prison about a church.

4TH SUPERVISOR (*opening the hatch*): Inspection!

WRZESNIK: Inspection!

TEMIROV: Everybody up!

They all line up along the cell in pairs, back to back. Rubin is at the end, nearest to the audience. Temirov in his Cossack cape marches along the line.

Any questions?

RUBIN: I have one.

TEMIROV: You're a clown. How many questions can one ask? Anyone else?

PRYANCHIKOV: I've got one. Why no food? What kind of treatment is that? Why did they shave our hair off?

TEMIROV: I'm sorry, but the block Inspector will rush through like a comet. If you want to get an answer, come and stand here, right in front of the door. (*He indicates a place next to Rubin.*)

RUBIN: Twaddle. My question is more important. I'll be speaking first.

Pryanchikov runs to change places with Temirov. The door crashes open. The block Inspector rushes in. The 6th Supervisor remains by the door. The Inspector walks past the line counting the pairs, first in one direction, then in another, amid complete silence, and is about to rush out again when first Rubin then Pryanchikov bar his way.

RUBIN: Citizen Inspector!

PRYANCHIKOV: Citizen! . . .

RUBIN: According to the rules, which are displayed . . .

PRYANCHIKOV: Citizen! . . .

RUBIN: The prisoners are allowed . . .

PRYANCHIKOV: But that's intolerable! . . .

RUBIN: To complain!

PRYANCHIKOV: To eat!

INSPECTOR (*unable to get away*): One at a time!

RUBIN (*raising his voice, with determination, pushing Pryanchikov aside, afraid that the Inspector will not hear him out*): I'm a victim of denunciation. I've been arrested quite illegally.

INSPECTOR (*with surprise*): So? What do you want?

RUBIN: My case is being conducted unfairly . . .

PRYANCHIKOV: The straw is rotten. It's disgusting to sleep on!

RUBIN: . . . I want to send a complaint to Beria . . .

PRYANCHIKOV: The slop bucket has no lid! Not hygienic!

RUBIN: Stop talking nonsense! To the Procurator General, to the National Judiciary . . .

PRYANCHIKOV: After all, we're not barbarians, Ethiopians. You must provide European conditions!

RUBIN: I need writing paper! I've been asking repeatedly and can't get it.

INSPECTOR: You will not get it!

He deftly moves round them and gets out through the door. Rubin runs after him.

RUBIN: By what right? . . .

The door is slammed shut, pushing Rubin inwards. The key is turned with a loud noise. The line breaks up.

TEMIROV: Now do you understand? Why don't you send your complaints to the Soviet Aviation Chemical Unit?

RUBIN (*attacking with clenched fists*): You and your sarcasms! . . . *They are separated.*

PRYANCHIKOV (*holding his head, in dead earnest*): What sort of country is this? Sheer lawlessness.

Klimov roars with laughter. The hatch is opened and we can see the head of the 6th Supervisor and the white overall of the dispenser.

6TH SUPERVISOR: Eighteen!

Two portions of bread are pushed through the hatch at a time. They are collected and put down on a coat which is spread out on the floor.

VOICES: Rations!

Our sacred props!

Temirov stands by the hatch and counts the rations. At the end he is also given sugar which he puts into a handkerchief. The hatch is banged shut.

TEMIROV: Fritz, share out the sugar.

Halberau takes the sugar, settles down comfortably, everybody brings his bits of paper, bits of cloth and, with the help of a spoon made out of a broken matchbox, he begins the ritual of sharing the sugar out. The door opens with a loud noise. An attendant in a dark overall enters carrying a wooden tub full of boiling water and a few empty one-litre tins which had contained American stew. He leaves. The door is shut.

VOICES: Boiling water!

SOMEONE (*having tried some*): It's cool already! Swill! Some boiling water!

Almost all have settled down in their places. Temirov and the Prisoner with a black eye are doling the food out. Mednikov is asleep once again.

PRISONER WITH A BLACK EYE: Who had the end bit yesterday?

TEMIROV: We got as far as here. (*He indicates, and starting from that place he doles out end bits of bread.*) Here you are. Here you are . . . (*Pryanchikov's turn comes. He stretches out his hand.*) Just you wait, sir. (*He by-passes him.*) You'll have to miss it this time. You're a novice. (*Having come to the end of the crusty bits, he shares out the middle bits.*) That's our custom . . .

PRYANCHIKOV (*sadly*): Do I get nothing?

TEMIROV: You'll get some, but the soft bit.

He gives him the last bit of bread. They are all eating it already. One of them is sawing it with a thread, others tear off tiny bits, still others bite minute mouthfuls and some have almost finished and are frenziedly chewing.

KULYBYSHEV (*muttering to himself*): A prisoner is entitled to four hundred and fifty grammes a day. Do with it what you like.

WRZESNIK: Drink your water, drink your water.

TEMIROV: According to the latest theories, a bucket of boiling water is equivalent to a hundred grammes of butter.

YELESHEV: They say a report has been sent to the Politburo. Approved at the highest level.

MOSTOVSHCHIKOV: How did they work it out?

KHOLUDENEV: It's to do with calories: after all, the water is hot, while the butter is cold.

KLIMOV: Marvellous!

DIVNICH (*standing up in the middle*): Gentlemen, I want to make a suggestion. Don't let us share out the sugar. Let's give our miserable grains to Leo for his birthday.

There is a confusion of sounds. Some come up to wish a Happy Birthday; others mutter.

[37]

PRISONER WITH A BLACK EYE: What – give away one's only ration?

PECHKUROV: There are no such regulations.

WRZESNIK: We've hardly anything to eat ourselves.

The hatch is slid open.

6TH SUPERVISOR: Letter M-ee!

DIVNICH (*decisively*): Aren't any!

6TH SUPERVISOR (*suspiciously*): None? (*Closes the hatch slowly.*)

RUBIN (*standing up*): Comrades, I'm most grateful, very touched, but of course I wouldn't dream of taking the sugar.

YELESHEV (*to Divnich*): We do have M's: Mednikov, Mostovshchikov. Why do you put us into this kind of situation? It doesn't do to irritate them.

DIVNICH (*finding it difficult to get a word in edgeways*): Their psychology, you see, is slavish. If they think they're Russians, let them sort the alphabet out!

MEDNIKOV (*rising, gobbling his rations*): The night interrogator went to bed, the day-time interrogator came to torture me . . . Dear friends, I feel I'm in for it.

DIVNICH: Gentlemen, we must rise above petty, selfish . . .

The hatch is slid open.

6TH SUPERVISOR: Who is there that starts with ee-eM?

DIVNICH (*sharply*): There's no such letter! We must be aware that this sap, these crumbs they give us, these eight grammes . . . (*the hatch is shut*) will not sweeten our existence. They've reduced us to the level of biological needs; they don't even call us political prisoners, which is something we could be proud of in this prison. This title has been sanctified over centuries. Don't let the Cheka take it away from us.

The hatch opens.

6TH SUPERVISOR: Who's here with the letter eM? E-m, I say!

MEDNIKOV: Mednikov.

6TH SUPERVISOR: So what are you playing at? Easy, now . . .

He shuts the hatch. Mednikov approaches the door. Halberau, shrugging his shoulders, collects all the sugar together and carries it onto the coat on which they shared out the bread.

RUBIN (*addressing everybody*): I'm most obliged. But if this sugar is for me, (*he fills two tins with the hot water, pours the sugar into both and stirs it with a crust of bread*) I am stirring two goblets; one goblet is for the one who has had no sleep for six nights (*passes it to Mednikov*) and the other is to go the rounds. (*He stirs.*)

VOICES: That's right.

That makes sense!

Bravo!

RUBIN (*taking a sip*): That's no water – it's a heavenly drink. Nectar!

MEDNIKOV (*drinks greedily*): Well, thank you friends. It's so gorgeously sweet I am truly restored. I feel almost drunk!

RUBIN (*slaps him on the back*): Hold out, Vasiliy! I hope you won't feel the beating …

The tin goes the rounds. The door opens with a grating noise.

6TH SUPERVISOR: Out!

Mednikov, his arms behind his back, leaves. The Supervisor, looking at his list:

6TH SUPERVISOR: Anyone with the letter Y?

YELESHEV: (*terrified*): Yeleshev …

6TH SUPERVISOR: Take your things!

YELESHEV: Me? Take my things?

The door is slammed shut.

YELESHEV: This is it. I'm finished! Quite finished!

TEMIROV (*to Pryanchikov*): Every morning they take people out of here. Some for a tribunal, some for a Special Disc.

PRYANCHIKOV: Special what?

KHOLUDENEV: Special Discussion. If they have nothing against you, no witnesses, no data, things are in a muddle …

YELESHEV (*gathering his possessions nervously*): How many years will they give me? I'm already an old man …

TEMIROV: Shame on you! You're only forty

KHOLUDENEV: You get sentenced behind your back.

PRYANCHIKOV: Do you mean – in your absence?

KHOLUDENEV: Millions of people coming here from Europe. To turn them round as quickly as possible, they have created a lottery where every ticket's a winner. Each ticket . . .

PRYANCHIKOV (*holding his head*): It's a nightmare!

KHOLUDENEV: Sign here please! Ten years. Greetings!

The door is being noisily unlocked. Yeleshev is all ready. He shovels the remains of his uneaten ration into his bag with some trepidation, embraces his companions quickly or shakes hands with some of them.

YELESHEV: Well friends! . . . Well, brothers! . . . Remember me kindly . . . If I upset anyone . . . hurt somebody . . .

DIVNICH: Good luck! Let all of us who shared the prison soup meet again in better times! (*He kisses him.*)

Yeleshev drags his bag towards the door, which opens at this moment. They all stand in a semi-circle to see him off, but a newcomer enters while the Supervisor makes a gesture towards Yeleshev to remain for a while. The door is locked again. The newcomer – Bolosnin – is tall, very thin, very pale. He is in uniform, but to start with it is not very clear which Army it belongs to. He is holding a small bundle, which contains all his belongings. Bolosnin straightens up with a kind of frenzied formality and looks at everyone.

VOICES: A newcomer!

Where from?

Are you from outside?

YELESHEV: There's an amnesty, they say. Know anything about it?

VOICES: He's silent.

Not a Russian, perhaps.

Shprechen Sie? . . .

Parlez-vous? . . .

Do you speak Engl? . . .

Bolosnin, with a smile of exhausted bliss, leans against the wall. He speaks slowly. His voice is weak but gains in strength as he, obviously, enjoys the luxury of speaking.

BOLOSNIN: No, not all . . . at once . . . I'm unused . . . to such a brilliant gathering, my friends. Twenty days and nights . . . twenty days and nights in a cell . . . and another . . . sixteen . . . in a solitary . . . Anybody want a smoke? Here – in this bundle . . .

He extends one hand with the bundle, made up of a handkerchief. The Prisoner with a black eye gets hold of the bundle eagerly. Wrzesnik and Pechkurov join him. They start rolling cigarettes. There is a mime of gestures in the cell as to how and who will smoke.

BOLOSNIN: I'm thirty years old, but I never thought it would be such happiness to be with other human beings.

YELESHEV (*faintly*): Amnesty? . . . Heard anything?

SOMEONE: He's got out of a *hold*, can't you understand? Out of a cell.

Klimov is downstage, kneeling. Having torn up some wadding from a padded jacket, he has rolled it up into a taper. With an air of someone very experienced, he begins to run it up and down with a sliver of wood over the floor. Bolosnin watches him with a pensive and enchanted smile.

BOLOSNIN: An ancient method of obtaining fire . . . Two bits of wood . . . A tinder . . .

YELESHEV: Please, please calm me down. They're waiting for me there! . . .

TEMIROV: He doesn't know, can't you see?

BOLOSNIN (*calmly*): It so happens . . . I do know.

RUBIN (*tense*): You're joking. You don't know.

BOLOSNIN (*very calmly*): That would have been a very cruel joke.

RUBIN: So there is?

YELESHEV: An amnesty?

KHOLUDENEV: I don't believe it!

DAVYDOV: Hurrah!

BOLOSNIN (*slowly*): I heard it myself on the radio while I was in the Investigator's office (*Everybody has gathered round him, listening avidly.*) In honour of our victory over Germany an

[41]

amnesty was announced yesterday – such as has never happened before.

DAVYDOV (*shaking his fists*): I told you so! Didn't I tell you?

YELESHEV: All these sentences are just to frighten us.

RUBIN: After all, it's a global victory!

BOLOSNIN: Amnesty, regardless of the length of sentence, is for thieves, speculators, swindlers, gangsters, deserters, civil and military plunderers, anyone who short-weighed, short-changed, or raped little girls. In short, the flower of the Soviet Union. The only ones not to be pardoned are former prisoners of war. (*They begin to disperse silently.*) Only those peasants who lived under the occupation, those who, under the Germans, went on working in factories, teachers who went on teaching (*Bolosnin gradually raises his voice as his anger grows*), only those who were sold out on the battlefield by a bunch of Generals. Only those who were forcibly driven into Germany. Only those who have individuality, think differently, have different views. So that Stalin's merciful hands have touched everyone, if you except the whole of the Russian people.

DAVYDOV (*triumphantly*): I'm free! I've been pardoned!

KLIMOV: Oh you dregs of human society in brown tatters! Go on, jump and skip. Why don't you shout 'Hop!'?

YELESHEV: O God! All is lost. I'm finished ... (*He sinks onto his bag.*)

MOSTOVSHCHIKOV: This is, truly, unheard of ...

KHOLUDENEV: What a typically Stalinist mocking manifesto!

GAI: And, no doubt, there's a lot of shouting and applause.

VOROTYNTSEV: Whose victory? Over whom? You mad nation! This victory is over you! ...

Everybody is motionless. Yeleshev alone goes out gloomily carrying his bag through the door which has been opened silently.

VOROTYNTSEV: May I introduce myself? (*He gives a military salute.*) Vorotyntsev, Colonel in the Russian Imperial Army.

Scene 2

BOLOSNIN (*in a similar manner*): Bolosnin, Ensign in the
  Russian Liberation Army. (*They shake hands.*)
  *Vorotyntsev then introduces all the other prisoners one by one, who
  shake hands with Bolosnin.*
VOROTYNTSEV: Kholudenev, Captain in the Red Army.
  Klimov, Soldier in the American Army.
  Temirov, Captain in the Royal Yugoslav Army.
  Halberau, Oberleutnant in the Wehrmacht.
  Wrzesnik, Lieutenant in the Polish Army.
  Fiacente, Corporal in the Italian Army.
  Pryanchikov, a fighter in the Belgian Resistance.
  Professor Mostovshchikov.
  Kuzma Kulybyshev, President of the Collective Farm
  named after Ivan Susanin . . .

Scene 3

A small room, the sun shines through the window. There is a large portrait of Stalin. Major Ognida and his typist Ninel sit side by side at a table.

OGNIDA (*dictating*): 'A Decree. I, Major Ognida, having examined and studied the anti-Soviet activities of Lieutenant-Colonel Alexander Ivanov of the Guards, which took the form: a) that in the period from 1941 to 1942 he slandered the planned retreat of the Red Army and attacked the unpreparedness of the Soviet Government for the war; b) that during 1944 he praised American war technology, as well as the part played by the Allies in the destruction of Hitler's Germany; c) that, having established personal contact under the guise of friendship with pilots of the American Air Force, George Fletcher . . . George Fletcher and William Rigby . . . William Rigby . . . , I have decided to cut short the intricacies of this investigation by arresting him. Signed, Major Ognida.' Full stop. Next.

NINEL: Do give me a bit of a rest, my arms are dropping off.

OGNIDA: Now, listen, Ninel, you are supposed to be the best typist in the department.

NINEL: Best typist, maybe, but I'm not a camel. Look, just look how much we have done since the morning.

OGNIDA: Splendid. When we get to half a hundred – we'll stop for a cigarette.

NINEL: But my fingers are numb. (*She stretches them out.*) Feel them – they're numb!

OGNIDA (*frowning, speaking rapidly*): Ninel! The Party, the Government and Comrade Stalin, personally, demand that we should *work*. Is that clear? Go on typing . . . 'I confirm . . .

Scene 3

(*Ninel types*) Deputy Commissar of State Security, Lieu-
tenant-General dot, dot, dot. Deputy Prosecutor of the
R.S.F.S.R., Major-General dot, dot, dot. A Decree. I, Major Ognida, having examined and studied the criminal, anti-
Soviet activities of Hero of the Soviet Union Lieutenant Ilya
Petrov, which found expression in the slanderous perversion
of Stalin's humane National policies in the regions of the
Volga, of the Crimea and of the Caucasus – I have decided to
cut short the intricacies of this investigation by arresting
him. Major Ognida.' Full stop. Next.

NINEL: I'm surprised at the amount you've found time to
write.

OGNIDA: During the night, Ninel, during the night.

NINEL: Tell that to the Marines! What patriotism! No sooner
do you get to Poland than you're surrounded by Polish girls.
As soon as you get to Germany – it's all the German ones.

OGNIDA: That's an old-established law of war time, Ninel –
all the girls of a vanquished nation belong to the conquerors.

NINEL: But Hilde is still a schoolgirl, she's only sixteen.

OGNIDA: Seventeen. And what's more, by private agreement,
her mother gets my rations.

NINEL: One could accuse you too of 'having established a
personal contact' . . . I remember the North-Western Front
. . . The local population had disappeared and you swarmed
all over us. I used to say to you then: Edward, I don't feel like
typing today. Do it yourself. And you used to sit down and
bash out: 'I, Lieutenant Ognida . . .'

OGNIDA: 'Have resolved, that the Deputy Commissar of the
National State . . .'

NINEL (*typing*): They used to ask me – Ninel? Ninel? Where
did you get such a wonderful name? Are you French? But
you know Ninel is only Lenin – backwards . . .

OGNIDA: 'A Decree. I, Major Ognida . . .'

NINEL: Let's make a change and do one about a woman . . .

OGNIDA: Don't fool around. The women's turn will come.

NINEL: Do you remember the story about this woman in

[45]

Oryol who got pregnant by a German Sergeant-Major, and
when our Army arrived, she hanged the baby and stuck a
note on him which said 'Death to the German Occupiers'.
(*She continues to type after Ognida's impatient gesture.*) . . .
Having examined and having looked into . . . I love it when
women are arrested . . . the criminal, anti-Soviet activities
. . . Why do they always arrest men? Always men . . . Your
approach is not statesmanlike.

OGNIDA: . . . the serving officer . . . Calm down. Nobody will
arrest you after your war service . . .

*Major Kapustin enters. He is plump and bouncy. He carries a
batch of papers. A Sergeant stops at the door.*

KAPUSTIN: Edward, listen.

OGNIDA: Well?

KAPUSTIN: I have to move you out of here for a couple of
hours.

OGNIDA: And why is that?

KAPUSTIN: I've got to read out the Instructions of the Special
Conference of the N.K.V.D.

OGNIDA: Why don't you go to Mironov's room?

KAPUSTIN: There's an interrogation going on in there.

OGNIDA: What about Vasiliy's?

KAPUSTIN: Another interrogation. I've been to all the offices
– they're all having interrogations.

OGNIDA: I'm short of time too. By seventeen hundred hours
I've got to get everything ready for signature.

KAPUSTIN: Well, I don't know. Rublyov told me to come
here. It's no joke. But we don't get enough time to announce
all the sentences, or to deport everybody on time, and the
General is due back today – you know what that means?

OGNIDA: It's a job and a half. You'll have to put forty people
in a cell instead of twenty. I must hurry with my batch.
They're walking about quite free.

KAPUSTIN: Go to the typing pool.

OGNIDA: But they've got ten typewriters going there, like so
many machine guns. It's unthinkable to work there.

KAPUSTIN: Well, go to the tower then. The tower is free.

OGNIDA: It stinks of rats. You go there yourself.

KAPUSTIN: We can't take the prisoners all the way up those stairs. What's more, the stairs haven't got safety grids. You go. Off with you.

OGNIDA: Oh, hell! No sooner do we get settled down ...

NINEL: I'm not going to carry the typewriter up those stairs.

OGNIDA: Are you expecting me to carry it for you?

KAPUSTIN: You can use my soldier. Stop squabbling. (*He makes a sign to the Sergeant. A Soldier enters.*) I shall be quick. (*Leafs through his thick file.*) You can come back in an hour and a half. (*The Soldier picks up the typewriter.*)

NINEL: Everybody's nervous, everybody's rushing around, all the papers will get mixed up. I hate these moves. (*She picks up the papers and hurries after the Soldier.*) Soldier, take care. There's one letter falling out!

She leaves, together with Ognida.

KAPUSTIN (*to the Sergeant*): Well, start shoving them in, according to the list. While one of them's here, you get the next one out of the cell. It'll go smoothly that way.

The Sergeant goes out. Kapustin arranges the table in his own way, spreads his papers out and throws open the window.

KAPUSTIN: Just look at this weather – sheer bliss. Wouldn't it be lovely to go fishing on the river, stay the night? Might get shot by the Germans, though ... Oh, what the hell. I won't be able to escape even on Sunday, there's so much work. They say that there's never been such a load of work, not even in 1937. (*He walks towards the table and yawns. Sidorov enters. He looks like a factory worker. He looks sullen. Kapustin, speaking through his yawn*): Name and surname?

SIDOROV: Mitrofan Sidorov.

KAPUSTIN: Date of birth?

SIDOROV: I never learned to write, Squire.

KAPUSTIN: What d'you mean – Squire? There have been no squires since the Revolution (*He rummages among the papers.*) Didn't you know? Born in 1895, is that right?

[47]

SIDOROV: That's how I'm registered.

KAPUSTIN (*indicating*): Sit down. (*Speaking in a rapid monotone*): 'By the decree of the Special Conference of the N.K.V.D. of the fifteenth of the sixth, 1945 Mitrofan Sidorov, born in 1895, is to be imprisoned in the corrective labour camp for ten years for having betrayed his country.' Sign here.

SIDOROV (*rising from the edge of his chair*): Comrade Major! The Germans took me away by force. How can I be guilty? . . .

KAPUSTIN: I've read it out to you – for betraying your country. Sign. Right here.

SIDOROV: Ten years. That's quite something . . . It's no good shoving it at me. I can't write, I've told you.

KAPUSTIN: Make a cross, then.

SIDOROV: I'm not going to do it. You make the cross.

KAPUSTIN (*writing*): On behalf of the illiterate . . .

SIDOROV: A five-cornered star . . .

KAPUSTIN: None of your lip. You're quite some illiterate, I see! Hullo! The next!

The Sergeant lets Yeleshev in.

KAPUSTIN: Name-surname-date-of-birth?

Sidorov leaves reluctantly, looking back. The Sergeant hurries him out.

YELESHEV: I'm a Moscow architect, fairly well known, a pupil of Shchusev . . .

KAPUSTIN: Who did you say? Shchukov?

YELESHEV: Do you mean my name? No. Yeleshev, Anatoliy. I was responsible for the building . . . (*He sits down.*)

KAPUSTIN: Date of birth?

YELESHEV: Mine?

KAPUSTIN: Naturally. I know my own.

YELESHEV: I'm forty. Born in 1904. If you've ever been to . . . you might have seen my building . . .

KAPUSTIN: Sit down. (*Reading in a rapid monotone*): 'By the decree of the Special Conference of the N.K.V.D. of the

fifteenth of the sixth 1945 the former soldier, Second Lieutenant of the Red Army Anatoliy Yeleshev, born in 1904, is to
be imprisoned in the corrective labour camp for ten years for
having betrayed his country.' Sign.

YELESHEV: Excuse me, from a strictly juridical point of
view . . .

KAPUSTIN: You can write about that from the camp. Sign.
Right here.

YELESHEV: You must hear me out, please. I yielded at the
interrogation, because I had hoped that in the course of the
trial, during cross-examination in court . . .

KAPUSTIN: It's for just such cross-examinations that we have
no time. Sign.

YELESHEV: I refuse to sign. It's monstrous! Who is the judge
here? Where's the court? Are you the court?

KAPUSTIN: I think I read it out to you clearly enough: a
Special Conference.

YELESHEV: But where is it?

KAPUSTIN: In Moscow.

YELESHEV: But how can it pass judgment on me when it has
never set eyes on me?

KAPUSTIN: Prisoner Yeleshev! I do not propose to explain
this to you. Sign.

YELESHEV (*with heat*): There is not a grain of truth in any of
the accusations in my case. It's like some fantastic novel.
The Investigator put down anything that came into his head,
and forced my signature by the threat of solitary confine-
ment, or danger to my family.

KAPUSTIN: So! You're even prepared to slander Soviet Investigations methods. Slander the Organs of State Security.
Your sentence obviously isn't long enough.

YELESHEV: No. Don't say that. But the verdict . . .

KAPUSTIN: This is not a verdict, but a decree. What you're
signing is the fact that you've read it.

YELESHEV (*with animation*): I never read it!

KAPUSTIN: Then say so. Here, read it, the devil take you! (*He*

throws the decree towards him, and lights a cigarette.) Only,
hurry up! Come on!

YELESHEV (*having read it*): Ten years! My God! I was thirty-
six years of age when I was taken prisoner of war. I shall leave
the camp as an old man of fifty. For what? For the fact that in
1941 officers floundered around like blind puppies without
maps, compasses or pistols.

KAPUSTIN (*in a rapid monotone*): It was your duty to die on the
field of battle. Sign.

YELESHEV: No! This is monstrous!

KAPUSTIN: Take care you don't regret it later on. (*Takes up
his pen.*) So-o . . . He refused to sign and expressed . . .

YELESHEV: No! I expressed nothing. I did not refuse!

KAPUSTIN: Then sign, blast you! You've wasted ten minutes
of my time.

YELESHEV: To the effect that I've actually read it?

KAPUSTIN: Well, yes, yes.

YELESHEV: But that doesn't mean that I accept the correct-
ness of the verdict or that I admit to being guilty.

KAPUSTIN: No, no, of course not.

YELESHEV: What about the amnesty?

KAPUSTIN: Yes, of course, there'll be an amnesty.

YELESHEV (*timidly*): There's been one? . . .

KAPUSTIN: There's been one, there'll be another. Everybody
will go free.

YELESHEV: Well, you put my mind at rest. (*He signs. Like a
king, who has abdicated his throne, he drops the pen in a state of
exhaustion.*) O my God. What is the price of human individuality?

KAPUSTIN: Hullo, there! Next!

*A little peasant, who looks like an illustration from a folk tale,
stands on the threshold, holding his fur hat in his hand. It is
Pakhomov.*

KAPUSTIN: Name? Surname?

YELESHEV (*without leaving his seat at the table*): We weren't
allowed any writing paper in our cells, so that we couldn't put

down our complaints or statements. If they do issue paper, it's tiny bits of blotting paper, so small you can't sign your name. I request that you give me an opportunity here, before I leave your study, to write an appeal on my case.

KAPUSTIN (*impatiently summoning Pakhomov*): Against regulations. (*To Pakhomov*): Name? Surname?

YELESHEV: How do you mean, regulations: What are the regulations?

SERGEANT (*pulling him off his chair and pushing him out*): Regulations are what we say they are. Out!

PAKHOMOV (*bowing*): Pakhomov, Theodore.

KAPUSTIN (*irritated by now*): Date of birth?

PAKHOMOV: 1901.

KAPUSTIN: Sign. (*Pakhomov signs.*) You may go. (*Pakhomov goes.*) Hullo! Next ... Hey you! Did I read it to you!

PAKHOMOV: Read what?

KAPUSTIN: What a fool! What did you sign then? Come here and sit down. 'The Decree of the Special Conference of the N.K.V.D. of the fifteenth of the sixth, 1945 states that Pakhomov, Theodore is to be imprisoned in the corrective labour camp for ten years for betraying his country; for undertaking an armed uprising; for working with the enemy and for contacts with world bourgeoisie; for undermining productivity in industry, agriculture and transport; for terrorist intentions, shortfall of provisions, as well as for connections which lead to suspicions of espionage.' Now, sign. (*Pakhomov takes up the pen.*) No, not again. (*Removes the pen.*) Is it clear?

PAKHOMOV (*looking enviously at a cigarette stub in the Major's mouth*): Permission to finish your cigarette, Comrade boss. (*Kapustin passes on the stub. Pakhomov bows deeply.*) God give you health, Comrade boss. (*Exit backwards, bowing, and pulling on the cigarette.*)

KAPUSTIN: Here, grandpa. (*He rapidly takes out a couple of cigarettes and offers them to Pakhomov who bows.*) Hullo! Next!

Scene 4

We can see, one by one, four investigation rooms which are absolutely identical as to size, position of the door and barred window, the desk of the Investigator, the position of the prisoner and the portrait of Stalin. It is only the Investigator and the prisoner who change, while the lights go out completely – to the tune of 'Stalin's Windmill'.

The tune of 'Stalin's Windmill'. The lights come up.

PART I

MYMRA AND KLIMOV

MYMRA: Question two. What was your rank and calling at the moment of being taken prisoner of war?

KLIMOV: Sergeant. In charge of the infantry section.

MYMRA (*writing down*): . . . of the infantry section. Question three (*absolutely expressionless*): What was your aim when you gave yourself up? Why didn't you shoot yourself?

KLIMOV: Terrific! Would you have done?

MYMRA: Prisoner Klimov. You are here to answer questions, not to ask them. You could be locked up in a cell for refusing to answer questions. Personally, we are ready to die for our leader. Question three: what was your aim when you gave yourself up? Why didn't you shoot yourself?

KLIMOV: I was waiting to see if the Divisional Commander would shoot himself first. However, he managed to escape to Moscow by 'plane out of the encirclement and then got promoted.

MYMRA (*writing down*): Answer. I gave myself up, my aim being to betray my Socialist country . . .

[52]

KLIMOV: We-ell, well; you can put it like that . . .
The lights go out. The tune of 'Stalin's Windmill'. The lights go up.

PART II

SVERBYOZHNIKOV AND PECHKUROV

SVERBYOZHNIKOV: Question two. What was your rank and calling at the moment of being taken prisoner of war?

PECHKUROV: What calling? I'm called Ivan. I humped an anti-tank gun about. I was number one.

SVERBYOZHNIKOV (*jumping up*): Don't you dare tell lies, you scum! Soviet Intelligence knows everything. I can see three yards into the ground beneath you! Commander of the Unit, eh? Did you remove your unit badge?

PECHKUROV: Ah, n-no. Didn't have a sickle, did I?

SVERBYOZHNIKOV: Not much of a soldier. Once a wild animal, always a wild animal, despite the training. A rich peasant's pampered son, maybe?

PECHKUROV: Agricultural labourers, both father and grand-father.

SVERBYOZHNIKOV: Soviet Intelligence knows everything! (*He sits down and writes.*) Question three. What was your aim when you gave yourself up? Why didn't you shoot yourself?

PECHKUROV: Ever seen an anti-tank gun? How do you think you can shoot yourself with that?

SVERBYOZHNIKOV (*getting angry*): You're getting insolent, you oaf. You had no arms? The Soviet Government was short of arms?

PECHKUROV: Don't know about the Government, but I carted the anti-tank gun without ammunition for a week.

SVERBYOZHNIKOV (*jumping up*): You snake! You vermin! We'll shoot you for this slander. We'll find a bullet for you; we'll order nine grammes to make a hole in your forehead! (*Returning to his desk he reads from a different piece of paper.*) 'I

[53]

gave myself up my aim being to betray my Socialist country.'
That's the sort of answer we want.
The lights go down. The tune of 'Stalin's Windmill'. The lights go up.

PART III

NEKLYUCHIMOV AND KULYBYSHEV

NEKLYUCHIMOV: Question two. What was your rank and calling at the moment of being taken prisoner of war?

KULYBYSHEV: What, in a penal company? I was there making up the numbers. I was working in the stables as the regimental goat.

NEKLYUCHIMOV (*laughing*): You funny old man ... Still, I've got to write something.

KULYBYSHEV: Well, if they demand to know my calling, write President of the collective farm named after Ivan Susanin.[4]

NEKLYUCHIMOV: Susanin? ... Wait a sec. Where did you say you come from?

KULYBYSHEV: How am I to answer that? Not too far from Kostroma.

NEKLYUCHIMOV: Oh I see. So Ivan Susanin and you are from the same district?

KULYBYSHEV: Fancy you knowing him. What a small world. Ivan, Michael, Theodore, Gleb – we're all from there. There's just one awkward thing – they're all Kulaks.

NEKLYUCHIMOV: How do you mean?

KULYBYSHEV: Simple. Under the Tsar, they gave them a pension. No wonder they become Kulaks.

NEKLYUCHIMOV: A pension?

KULYBYSHEV: They must have obliged somehow, see. Now. In the 'thirties they got dispossessed, packed off to Siberia. Not a squeak from them for six years, so in our fervour we name our collective farm 'Lenin's Path' – but in '36 we get a piece of paper, which says Ivan Susanin was your respected fellow-citizen and you are to call your farm after him. Well, we'd nothing against that, the Government knows best. On the other hand, we're a bit ashamed before our neighbours. It would have been all right if they'd told us to call it after Michael or Theodore or his brothers. But Ivan, of all of them, was the most useless – he drank and rioted and brawled. To hell with him! Still, I suppose he managed to get to the top . . .

While he is talking Neklyuchimov has taken a plate of sandwiches out of his drawer.

NEKLYUCHIMOV: Oh dear, Kuzma, you're a nice old man, you know. It's a shame that you got yourself into a prisoner of war camp. Here, have one. (*Kulybyshev takes a sandwich, sniffs it and puts it back on the plate.*) Why don't you eat it? It can't be that you're not hungry.

KULYBYSHEV: Why . . .

NEKLYUCHIMOV: Eat, then! Eat as much as you can. I can't give it to you in your cell, but you can eat here. (*Looks at Kulybyshev intently.*) Wait a minute. Why are you refusing to eat?

KULYBYSHEV: Well, you see . . . I don't want to upset you, truly . . . But . . . perhaps . . . it's poisoned.

NEKLYUCHIMOV: Kuzma, Kuzma! (*He is hurt.*) Do I look like someone who'd poison? (*He looks at himself in the open window pane, as if it were a mirror.*) Eh? We-ell . . . Let me take the one you're worried about. I'll eat it myself.

Kulybyshev indicates the sandwich. Neklyuchimov eats it and walks towards his desk. Kulybyshev eats also.

NEKLYUCHIMOV: Last time . . . you told me about how the penal company crossed the Dniepr on logs . . . and how some were shot and others fell off and were drowned; and how only a handful of you managed to clamber up the steep banks, but were taken prisoner . . . So, now, question three: what was your aim in giving yourselves up? Why didn't you shoot yourselves? (*Kulybyshev is eating his sandwiches hungrily.*

Neklyuchimov writes): Answer. I gave myself up my aim being
to betray my Socialist country.
The lights go down. The tune of the 'Windmill'. The lights go up.

PART IV

KAMCHUZHNAYA AND POSVYANTSEVA

KAMCHUZHNAYA: Here. This is for Anastasiya Posvyantseva. This letter was found in the pocket of the dead man's
jacket.

POSVYANTSEVA: Give it to me! Give it to me!

KAMCHUZHNAYA: That depends on your behaviour. (*Skims
through the letter.*) 'Anastasiya, my love . . . Whatever I do,
wherever I am, my thoughts . . .' There are pages and pages
of sweet nothings here.

POSVYANTSEVA: Listen to me, Captain Kamchuzhnaya! . . .

KAMCHUZHNAYA: 'The lands around Oryol disappear from
beneath our very feet . . .' That's sufficiently straightfor-
ward. 'We are retreating, in order to take up defences at
Oryol itself. Oh, the blue-green stalks of wheat all blackened
by the blast of bomb explosions . . .' Quite a poet, isn't he?
. . . 'No, we will not surrender the town . . .' He's quite an
educated little officer, that husband of yours, I see . . . 'But
since you're ten miles from the front your life will be in
danger. I beg you to go to our relatives in Saxony . . .' Well,
he begged unnecessarily. You'd thought of it yourself . . . By
the way, there's a postscript here in someone else's handwriting. Whose is it, eh?

POSVYANTSEVA: I can't see.

KAMCHUZHNAYA (*approaches, showing it*): Here.

POSVYANTSEVA: I can't see when someone else is holding it.
Let me take it.

KAMCHUZHNAYA (*with a sneer*): Don't think you can fool
me, you idiot. This is Captain Theodore Kolosovitov's
handwriting! Did he come to your house?

POSVYANTSEVA: No.

Scene 4

KAMCHUZHNAYA: What about Ensign Igor Bolosnin?

POSVYANTSEVA: I don't remember.

KAMCHUZHNAYA (*holding the letter in front of Posvyantseva's face*): You'll soon be able to read the whole letter. It is the *last* letter from your husband! There are eight pages of it. Eight tender pages. What do you know about Igor Bolosnin?

POSVYANTSEVA: Bolosnin? I don't remember.

The light goes out.

Scene 5: A Flashback

In the light of the setting sun we can see a small garden, which contains a single-storey house with a summer terrace. There is a table fixed to the ground and some benches.

A bell tolls intermittently.

Anastasiya is laying the table, putting on a cloth and placing tea cups. Bolosnin, who is wearing a German uniform, has a badge on the sleeve which says 'R.L.A.' (Russian Liberation Army)

BOLOSNIN: They are ringing the bell. They are ringing for Vespers . . . O Russia, can this ever come back again? Will you ever be yourself? I have lived on your soil for twenty-six years, I spoke Russian, listened to Russian, but never knew what you were, my country! . . .

ANASTASIYA: And you, yourself, where are you from Igor?

BOLOSNIN (*unloading food from a basket*): I come from, I'm a citizen of a town which I'm so fond of I don't know what a suitable name for it would be. Saint . . . ? That got lost long ago. Especially since this town was not named after any apostle. Petersburg – that's German. Petrograd? – I don't see that name making Russia rear up under the reins of Peter the Great.[5] This town does not belong to Pushkin, or to Dostoyevsky. There is no one name that would cover it in full. To myself I call it . . . shall I tell you?

ANASTASIYA: What?

BOLOSNIN: I call it No-grad. I'm a citizen of a No-grad.

ANASTASIYA: No-grad. That sounds like the Novgorod that never was. It has a very Russian sound. You know those fragrant Russian words which have a stress on the first syllable?

BOLOSNIN: Added to which, it is completely correct. There

is no other large city on the Neva. (*A pause.*) My father is there. He's a high-ranking officer – a General. They used to spoil me, they thought of giving me a car before the war . . . O Lord, how hard it is to realise at the age of twenty-five how blind one's been, how blind and insignificant! In the louse-ridden prisoner of war camps, to be rejected by one's country, to be horrified by one's shameful Komsomol youth! . . .

ANASTASIYA: You know, Igor, I have a brother not far from Leningrad – on the other side . . . He's in the artillery too. Very young. His last letter came from Pulkovo, but was unfinished. While my husband is now here . . . What is the truth? How will it all end? . . . (*A pause. The tolling of the bell speeds up and then stops.*) My husband used to say – you two are fine, only your outlook on life is too gloomy.

BOLOSNIN: Was anyone unkind to him? They had told him all sorts of rosy things about Russia while he was abroad. (*He opens the wine bottles and the conserves.*) It's silly to go on repeating that the White Army consisted of landowners. My father, for instance, came of an aristocratic family, but goodness knows why he joined the Bolsheviks, while your husband's father was a simple telegraphist, not a member of the nobility, had no money and yet spent the whole Civil War in the White Army; took his wife and children down south, retreated to Gallipoli and did not stay in Red Soviet Russia . . . Incidentally, they told me, while I was visiting them in Saxony, that Vsevolod's elder sister went to school where . . .

ANASTASIYA: Yes, where my mother was the headmistress. They come from Oryol.

BOLOSNIN: Then, both you and your mother are teachers. And both teaching Russian language and literature . . . (*Anastasiya nods.*) I met so many nice people during those two years when I stopped being a Soviet citizen, they were so generous and we understood one another so well . . .

KOLOSOVITOV (*in the same uniform as Bolosnin; he is huge. He wears glasses and carries a book. As he comes down from the terrace he is humming*):

> O, Anastasiya, you flourished here,
> You sang your songs,
> You wove carpets for me, your groom,
> But where are you now? . . .

ANASTASIYA: Theodore, take off your glasses when you're with me. They ruin your image.

KOLOSOVITOV: What's one to do, Anastasiya? There are no more giants in the twentieth century. I have put Alexei Tolstoy back on the shelf, but have borrowed Herzen. Is that all right? (*He takes off his glasses*).

BOLOSNIN: Why Herzen? He's not your kind of thing.

KOLOSOVITOV: Why not? He was an extremely intelligent fellow. Do you know what he called Marx, *et al*? A *sulphuric band*! He does not belong to the Bolsheviks. Just bear that in mind. We might yet have to start publishing *The Bell*,[6] you know.

ANASTASIYA: You have hundreds of plans, Theodore. And look at all the things you've brought. (*She walks back to the house with a purposeful air.*)

KOLOSOVITOV: There's one plan, the most important one, I never completed. I didn't stamp out Stalin.

BOLOSNIN (*staggered*): Were you intending to?!

KOLOSOVITOV: Why do we have to suffer him? Don't you see, Igor, my life's been like a rolling stone. I've been all over Mother Russia: to the Aldan and the Yenissey, to Chukotka and to the Kolyma, and Norilsk, and even to places where bears never get to – I got as far as that. I've been going round as a research geologist ever since 1926. But let me tell you this extraordinary thing – I come to a place for the first time and there's nothing there; I come a second time and there's a camp there. Camps, camps, camps, nothing but camps. Entire continents behind barbed wire – GULAG ARCHIPELAGO. Nothing left of Russia! All roads were barred, I felt enmeshed in that blasted barbed wire. I wanted to walk straight through it, tearing it up, tearing it up. And the people I had to work with! It was either a camp prisoner under guard, or a camp prisoner without a guard, either a former prisoner or a future one. It was desperate; what was one to do? To organise a political party? Some underground movement? But there were no real people left, just a lowing herd; all the G.P.U. herdsman had to do was to crack his whip for them all to fall on their front legs. And a thought occurred to me that I might knock off the pock-marked cretin responsible for it all myself. It was just then that I published a book on geology, got transferred to Moscow, became known; was taken up by the Academy, became a member of the All-Union Society for Cultural Relations with Foreign Countries. They held receptions close by the Kremlin. 'The Father of all the Peoples, the Leading Light of all the Sciences would be around'. Glory to the old Blackcock with his feathered feet! Of course, within the Kremlin it would have been more resounding – there's resonance there, but I examined all the country houses.

BOLOSNIN: But it's impossible to take any arms into the Kremlin. One's searched a hundred times. It's tricky.

KOLOSOVITOV: Tricky things are for tricksters. What the hell did I need arms for? *These* are my arms. (*He stretches out his two hands.*) All I needed was to find myself within ten paces of him and, in some cold place, one leap ... But there's another problem. They say he has at least six doubles ...

BOLOSNIN: Just think! It's possible you weren't alone; maybe there were a half dozen like-minded people milling around him, not knowing one another – and not one got within reach!

KOLOSOVITOV: I would have reached him. As a schoolboy of fourteen I experienced gun-fire and got gassed in Yaroslavl – they used to shoot chemical shells at us then. The Cheka shot me, but I survived. I would have waited, if necessary, till I became an old Academician to get within reach – but the war came ... Stalin went East from Moscow and I, after some thought, decided to go West for the time being. Just then they were recruiting for the Home Guard among the Academicians ...

BOLOSNIN: From the Academy of Sciences? From there into the Home Guard?

KOLOSOVITOV: Indeed, yes. Full speed. Everybody wanted to show off, nobody wanted to be left behind. Everyone signed on. Later on the party bosses were transferred to the rear to form the nucleus of scientific cadres, but those of us who weren't quite so good – off to the wars with us. We were beaten hollow at Vyazma ... Kulik, for instance, you know – the famous Siberian astronomer – he was in my company. He died in a prisoner of war camp; Kachalov's son also. I can't enumerate them all ... The prisoner of war camp! D'you know, Igor, I expected all sorts of vile, low-down tricks from the Bolshevik government, but I didn't expect that it would betray its own prisoners of war!

BOLOSNIN (*very agitated*): Don't talk to me about that, Theodore! In two hundred years time I will be croaking from my grave about those Russian prisoners! In there I survived typhus, hunger; my love for the Revolution died there, my love for my father and my faith in man nearly disappeared there! They beat each other over the head with sticks, with mess tins to get some of that miserable soup, that filthy prison soup; ten thousand of them queuing up, starting at midnight. They used to gnaw tree-bark to the last shred. And then we are told that we are traitors to our own country. The swine, they should be put in there! The English, the French, the Serbs, the Norwegians – all prisoners of war like us – were our neighbours behind the barbed wire. They received their pay-packets for the years in prison, they received rewards for their years of service, promotion, letters from home, parcels from the Red Cross. They didn't even have to queue for the German soup cauldron and threw chocolates and cigarettes to us over the fence.

Scene 5: A Flashback

Vsevolod, wearing the same uniform, comes from round the corner of the house, carrying a samovar with a teapot on top.

BOLOSNIN: Only 'Ivan' is unwanted in the world, only 'Ivan' belongs to no one. How can Stalin be forgiven for that?

KOLOSOVITOV: But, Igor, all of them, every one of them were like that. All those Lenins and Tomskys, Trotskys and Shchatskys. What did they care if it was Russia, or Mexico? – they didn't have to wear prison clothes.

VSEVOLOD: And did you imagine, gentlemen, that our émigré leaders were any brighter? Do you think they would bother to consult the Russian people? Not a chance! Each one of them could only go on repeating that he had been right. They did not care that some fifteen, twenty years had passed during which time the nation suffered, grew up, had its own thoughts. How we argued with them! And we left them! A new movement arose among us, the younger ones. It was against *pre-deter-min-ation*. We do not force our decisions on the people. We intend to free the people, but since the burden was not carried by us, it is not up to us to decide how: to the point that if the Russian peasant likes his collective farm, let him have it. If the Ukraine wants to become separate – let it. As to Georgia – the time is long past for it to go its own way. At least, that way, we wouldn't be governed and marketed by Georgians. Our motto was: better less, but better! Do we need territories, friends! God gave us a lot of land. What we need is loving rulers, stable laws . . . (*He is out of breath.*)

We can see Anastasiya on the terrace in a different dress.

ANASTASIYA: Comrades . . . uhum . . . Gentlemen! It's so good of you to come. The best kind of party is an unexpected one. Do sit down, or the samovar will get cold.

They settle down.

KOLOSOVITOV: O samovar, O pot-bellied urn! How you have been reviled by the enemies of mediocrity – by all the Chekhovs, the Gorkys, the Kuprins. There they go on the stage for three hours on end and putting on airs and

[63]

wailing: we're summer folk, we're bungalow dwellers! But what's wrong with that? Gentlemen, I drink to the middle classes.

BOLOSNIN: Me too. Food, drink, love, home, the upbringing of children have all been declared shameful activities. That's not progress, it's Bedlam. They should try living in hostels building Communism.

KOLOSOVITOV: Into camps with them! Onto a transport train, onto the top bunk! (*Holding a bottle in one hand.*) I hope, Anastasiya, you'll allow me just one toast. Only one, because now we find ourselves in a pure feminine world; thereafter we shall be drinking tea with milk. Anastasiya, I want to express my admiration for the noble work you are doing. For two years now, in a Russian school, which is situated at a hair's breadth distance from Soviet Russia and a Russia whose future is unknown, you have been unfolding before children the beauties of our language, the might of our literature, the joyless history of our people. And you've been doing that, not through official text books, but guided by your own conscience and sense of truth. At the moment we are killing Russians, for no good purpose, while you're bringing them up for the future. I want to thank you and others like you, dear Anastasiya. Your good health! (*They drink.*)

ANASTASIYA: Thank you . . . Thank you, Theodore. You're a great support to me. The times are so strange, they hang heavily, just now. Over there, near Bryansk, schools are being burned down by partisans, while here in Oryol we get anonymous letters, telling us not to dare to teach anything while we are under German occupation, or we'll pay for it. What sort of drunken louts write such letters? Are they afraid that children will grow up all wrong, not to mention that they'd lost not just months, but years of schooling. It's not their fault. If a child leaves his school desk, he will never return to it . . . I wish you knew how difficult I find it all! (*She bows her head.*)

Scene 5: A Flashback

KOLOSOVITOV (*humming*):

> You languished and pined in your room,
> While I, in my powdered wig,
> Went to pay my respects to the queen
> And never saw you again ...

ANASTASIYA: What crude and unfeeling barbarians! How can I stop teaching? After a day's work, I come home refreshed, excited, so happy, I can hardly get to sleep. Before 1941 we had this continuous indoctrination. We had to mouth some class-ridden rubbish about the petty-bourgeois, who'd gone mad. We had to expose some bad moment in history about this or that; to throw Don Quixote into the rubbish bin of history; had to say that the poet, limited by his gentry background couldn't quite grasp ... Leo Tolstoy, according to them, couldn't quite grasp, while some Kirpotin grasps everything! ... But, at least, there was a sense of certainty, however stifling, of some permanence, however bad. But now everything is topsy-turvy. The official pecking order of prescribed quotations has gone, everything is in flux, you don't know what to serve with what – no one knows, teach any way you like; the Dostoyevsky once forbidden is now available – but I can now teach from the heart. I have grown wings. The trouble is, I have no cushion of air to lift me up. There's no firm ground either, come to that. What's going to happen? And how?

VSEVOLOD (*squinting at the sunset*): Look at these luminous clouds. And as soon as the sun sets, it will be like it is on the front line – a warm, bright west and a gloomy, threatening east. (*To Anastasiya*): Our dug-out faces east. How severe the east becomes after the sun has set – I never noticed it before, because we tend to admire the sunset ... There's some specially bitter charm in this spring of 1943. The Oryol-Kursk line lies on the map like a huge question mark. It is still, like a sleeping snake and no one knows where its tail will strike. Here, three miles from the front line, we have kitchen gardens, the wheat's growing, villages full of people;

[65]

and over there for twenty miles everybody's been chased out, no one lives there, nothing grows apart from steppe grasses, wild flowers and thistles, as in the days of Batiy.[7] But both they and we are on the same mid-Russian lands – hills, sparkling gullies, the waving green foliage of woods, and the nightingales, nightingales at night! . . . The region of Oryol. The dream of my childhood. I wouldn't mind dying in a place like this, truly.

ANASTASIYA: Don't even think it. The very thought might make it happen.

VSEVOLOD: After it has grown dark, for a short time there are no rockets, no rattle of machine guns, the lonely nocturnal Henschels do not drone – the wild grasses are fragrant over the battle front . . . O Anastasiya, come with us there for a day. It's worth visiting! . . .

ANASTASIYA: I shall, I shall certainly come with you. May I Theodore?

KOLOSOVITOV: Better not, Anastasiya. Here we appear to you like some kind of knights in shining armour, we come here all fresh, we speak of beautiful things, while over there we drink and drink and drink, our eyes pewter-coloured, we play cards . . . It's better not!

ANASTASIYA: But why so? When you're in this house you're not like that?

VSEVOLOD: I don't know why they behave like that. I never drink.

BOLOSNIN: But what's one to do? – just consider. I stopped at a cottage in Stanovoy Kolodez and got to talking with the peasant woman. She said: 'God only knows what sort of person you are – you seem to be neither Russian nor German.' That's the horror of it – during the course of this war, in the eyes of ordinary people, it is the Bolsheviks who have usurped the right to be called Russian. And indeed, to look at us from outside in – we are a suspect lot of companies, inserted into the Wehrmacht. Where here would you find independent, solidly Russian regiments, divisions? Our own sections of the battle front?

VSEVOLOD: But we could have marched on, given the chance. Boy, how we would have marched! Like an avalanche, ever increasing, growing ... Some three hundred versts to Moscow, through towns and villages – there would have been flowers, caps tossed into the air, embroidered towels!

KOLOSOVITOV: Those towels, Vsevolod, are now worn to a frazzle; as to caps, people treasure them.

BOLOSNIN: What sort of uniforms are we wearing? What are we fighting for? This military jacket is burning on my back! I'm as ashamed of the German eagle as I would have been of the Red star! ... What is it that we are doing? Side by side with the German soldiers, we're killing Russians so as to liberate the Russians! That's how far we've been cornered. On my latest assignment I've been introduced to General Vlasov.[8] He wanted to know about morale at the front. I told him straight out: we cannot see any other Russian governments emerging, in our heart of hearts we consider the Anglo-Saxons our true allies, but in the meantime, to the wonder of the S.S., we're aiding and abetting Hitler.

KOLOSOVITOV: Do you know, Igor, the devil himself tried to brew beer with the English but had to refuse their malt.

ANASTASIYA: So what did Vlasov say?

BOLOSNIN: He flinched. I have a feeling that he's rather confused. Bitten off more than he can chew.

KOLOSOVITOV: Well, of course, no leader in Vlasov's position can do a damn thing.

VSEVOLOD: Then what did he start it all for? And why does he go on dragging it out, this muddle? Why does he encourage, deceive so many ardent young lives?

KOLOSOVITOV: But what are these ardent young ones to do, anyway? Die off in prisoner of war camps? He's doing right. You either get hanged or cut the noose.

BOLOSNIN: There's just one hope: to join up with the Allies even if it is only at Hitler's death.

VSEVOLOD: Then why don't we issue an ultimatum to Hitler! We should demand . . .

KOLOSOVITOV: . . . squeeze a drop of water out of a stone! That wasn't the way to fight the Bolsheviks. It's easy to see what we should have done: we should have landed forces outside the labour camps! All one needed do then was to knock out the miserable camp guards and hungry hands would be stretching out for armaments. We would have had an army twelve-million-strong, and in the rear, what's more. But Hitler, that arrogant idiot who imagined he could conquer Russia without Russian help and against the Russians – he more or less continued with the collective farms, he burnt down villages, he was afraid to create independent regiments from us. No wonder the Kremlin moustachio is rubbing his hands – there's a know-nothing in the world even thicker than him! Hitler won't understand even on his deathbed that the Russian Liberation Army[9] was the fulcrum to overthrow . . .

ANASTASIYA (*fixedly*): *Was*? Theodore – why *was*?
It is getting quite dark.

BOLOSNIN: If the new Russia is to be created by Hitler – to hell with such a Russia!
It is quite dark. The tune of 'Stalin's Windmill'. The lights go up. We are back in the investigation room.

KAMCHUZHNAYA: And do you imagine that your romantic little garden had not been surveyed and bugged by honest Soviet patriots? What about Bolosnin? Lieutenant Igor Bolosnin?

POSVYANTSEVA: I don't remember.

KAMCHUZHNAYA: You don't remember, you slut! What if I bring him in?

POSVYANTSEVA: Go on, then.

KAMCHUZHNAYA: And Kolosovitov as well?

Scene 5: A Flashback

POSVYANTSEVA: You won't be able to get them. Your N.K.V.D.'s arms are too short.

KAMCHUZHNAYA: Go on, kneel, you filth, kneel! (*She pushes her into a corner onto her knees.*)

The lights go out. The Windmill melody. The lights come up.

Scene 4 (resumed)

PART V

MYMRA AND KLIMOV

MYMRA: Question six. Who gave you the task of developing spying activities in the Soviet Union?

KLIMOV: That's something new. I never studied in a spy college.

MYMRA (*in level tones*): Don't try to confuse the investigation. You did serve in the American Army from 1944?

KLIMOV: Yes, I did serve with the Allies.

MYMRA: The fact that it was with the Allies is of no importance. Did they not rope you in?

KLIMOV: How do you mean? The very fact that I served?

MYMRA: O.K. As an American soldier you could have got a passport to the U.S.A., or Canada, or . . .

KLIMOV: Anywhere at all.

MYMRA: Now *you* are confused. How, then, do you explain your voluntary return to your country?

KLIMOV: How . . . do I explain . . . my voluntary . . . ?

MYMRA (*nods and writes with glee*): Answer. In some confusion . . . I testified untruthfully. I was given a task by American Intelligence.

The lights go out. The Windmill melody. The lights come up.

PART VI

SVERBYOZHNIKOV AND PECHKUROV

SVERBYOZHNIKOV (*writing*): Answer. I was given a task by American Intelligence.

Scene 4 (resumed)

PECHKUROV: Citizen Investigator! I've never set my eyes on any Americans. I was liberated by our own people.

SVERBYOZHNIKOV: Who's *ours*? Who's *yours*? *Yours* are running around on all fours in the Krasnoyarsk region of Siberia. (*A pause.*) Well, O.K. Let's say by American Intelligence through an officer of the German Army . . . what was his name?

PECHKUROV: Whose?

SVERBYOZHNIKOV (*writes*): Richard Bauer. (*Rubbing his hands.*) There, now. The charge sheet's complete! (*He sorts out his papers, humming*): 'But he who marches through life with a song . . .' Hey, do you get enough grub over there?

PECHKUROV: Enough, my foot! A piece of bread this small and a couple of half-full tins of prison soup . . .

SVERBYOZHNIKOV (*brings the charge sheet and a pen dipped in ink to Pechkurov's table*): I'll tell them to give you extra food; you'll be getting some gruel and a hundred grammes of bread. Here, sign.

PECHKUROV: I refuse. It's all a tissue of lies.

SVERBYOZHNIKOV: You carion! Who taught you to give answers like that?

PECHKUROV: I taught myself.

SVERBYOZHNIKOV: Not taught enough. You've not yet sat on a steel hedgehog. (*Advancing slowly.*) You've so far been eating boiled corn and had quiet nights. You wait till we scramble your balls like so many eggs. Would you like that?

PECHKUROV (*downcast*): Well, governor, if I'm to die, then I'm to die. I'm fed up and tired of this whole business. I've no wish to live.

SVERBYOZHNIKOV (*stops, flabbergasted*): What? No wish to live, you son of a bitch?

PECHKUROV (*peaceably*): That's right, no wish to live. You occupy a nice cosy niche, see, you have it off with girls, so you want to live – and you think everybody's the same. But no, I've been through it these last five years. If I'm to get another ten – there's no point in living.

SVERBYOZHNIKOV (*at a loss*): Hum. That's psychologically decadent. How can you not want to live? (*Becoming animated*): You speak with a voice that's not your own. Soviet Intelligence knows everything. You've been taken out of your isolation cell too soon. I didn't want to do it, but I'll have to remove your old Mum and Dad from Smolensk and pack them off to Siberia ...

PECHKUROV (*calmly*): We'll thank you for that. Perchance, there are no collective farms there.

SVERBYOZHNIKOV (*utterly at a loss*): Hell's teeth! What am I to do with you, you reptile?

The lights go out. The Windmill melody, which stops, as if the record got stuck. The lights go up.

PART VII

NEKLYUCHIMOV AND KULYBYSHEV

NEKLYUCHIMOV: Question six. Who instructed you to organise a spy network within the Soviet Union? Eh? Old man. Eh? (*He laughs.*) Who gave you this assignment? (*He laughs louder and Kulybyshev joins him. The laughter increases.*) Eh? You mole? (*They laugh.*) Answer. I was recruited by American Intelligence. Why aren't you eating? Do finish.

KULYBYSHEV: I've eaten my fill,
Sufficient to kill.
I must take rest
And recover my zest.

NEKLYUCHIMOV: Always joking, eh? You're a cheerful soul.

KULYBYSHEV: Were it not for the frosts,
The hop plants would grow –
Maybe fast, maybe slow –
But as tall as these posts.

NEKLYUCHIMOV: (*moving to sit down closer to Kulybyshev, in a confidential tone*): All right, Kuzma, let's leave all that aside. Tell me, rather, what it was like working for a *Bauer* as a farm labourer.

KULYBYSHEV: Eh, m'dear. Let's say, that wherever there's plenty, your life's O.K. This word – *Bauer* – it means a peasant, but just go into their cellars, or climb up into the attics! From one summer to another – there are apples THIS size! And the grapes, and the wine . . . They gave me a litre a day – to drink as you please . . . Just consider, what kind of village is it if the houses are two storeys high, built of brick? You wake up in the morning under your feather bed and you lament – Kuzma, you're a slave. Talk of cattle, or poultry in the farmyard . . . As old men of the village used to say, you may be living under a yoke, but you're still well off. Well, then they sent us beyond the Rhine into the trenches – and I found myself with the Americans. A Russky, they said, a Russky! So I looks around and I likes it there, too. The Germans are bright, but the Americans are even brighter. They value people more than possessions. But the Russian seems to be under an evil spell. He may visit every black-smith's in the region and yet returns without a horseshoe. He's got a longing to go back to his own place. Shall we ever see it? They entice you: 'Come back, little lamb, come back!' And when you are back: 'Here's the big bad wolf'.

NEKLYUCHIMOV: There you go, old man, there you go. You're saying these things to me! – to the Investigator of State Security. Should we let you go back to your Kostroma region, what sort of things would you be saying there? Who would want to work in the collective farms after hearing your kind of stories? You must admit that's true.

KULYBYSHEV: I s'pose, it's true . . .

NEKLYUCHIMOV: Well, there you are, as you see. I can't let you off, old thing. You're being imprisoned not because of you, whether you're guilty or not; it's because you've seen things, do you understand, it's because you've seen things! But whatever's written in this charge sheet – makes no odds. (*A pause.*) So, that's your choice: if you sign now, you'll be sent into a camp, you'll work there, you'll get your kilo of rations – and look, you've done your ten years and come back to the old woman. But if you don't – I get a reprimand, but then I've had lots of them and I'm used to it, but you'd be passed on to another Investigator, and you'd be kept miserable in a cell, and getting only three hundred grammes and no hot food – and you'd come crawling on all fours: let me have the charge sheet, let me sign! . . . So, why don't you take pity on yourself? (*He brings over the sheet and the fountain pen.*) Come on, old man, scribble your name, go on, scribble. 'I was recruited by American Intelligence.'

Kulybyshev rubs his head. He signs, his lips moving. The lights go out. The Windmill melody. The lights go up.

PART VIII

KAMCHUZHNAYA AND POSVYANTSEVA

Posvyantseva is in the corner on her knees. Kamchuzhnaya is sitting on a couch.

KAMCHUZHNAYA: Do you know, Your Highness, I can't understand your grief. While you're a strong and lusty female – your life's in your own hands, wherever you are. In any camp you can get men, any your heart desires. Should you find yourself in a men's camp centre, you'll get the red carpet treatment, you silly fool! I envy you in some ways, would you believe? Get up! I'm talking sense.

POSVYANTSEVA (*rising*): All I ask is that the child should be given to her grandmother. What a disaster it was that I was arrested on my way home. They could have done it when I got there.

KAMCHUZHNAYA: We might do that. Although, perhaps, your daughter would be brought up better by the State. She will grow up a true patriot, will not get married to the first émigré bandit and will not go off to Saxony.

POSVYANTSEVA: I'm not the only one brought up here. My brother was too and he's an officer in the Red Army.

KAMCHUZHNAYA: Well, who knows. He may be a traitor too. We'll have to look into that. (*Changing her attitude sharply.*) He's been killed! Your brother's been killed in East Prussia, he's been killed by the friends of your husband, he's been killed by Vlasov's Army!

POSVYANTSEVA: He's alive!

KAMCHUZHNAYA (*jumps up, sorting papers on the table*): Here, read this. Go on, read it! He found himself surrounded, was killed in the village of Orendorf, having heroically spent all his bullets in an unequal struggle.

Posvyantseva, having read it, weeps.

KAMCHUZHNAYA (*standing next to her, tenderly*): Anastasiya, my dear, who did you get tangled up with? What sort of mire did you descend into? All these Kolosovitovs, and all these Bolosnins! An empty, amoral lot, who have nothing to recommend them but hatred. You do understand it now?

POSVYANTSEVA (*lifting her head, no longer weeping*): Yes, I do understand it now. I have understood, within these walls, that if my brother had survived, if he had escaped from the encirclement, you wouldn't have believed him, you would have asked him why it was that he wanted to return to his country voluntarily, you'd have torn off his epaulettes and given him ten years!

KAMCHUZHNAYA (*in a monotone*): How come you're so clever? How come you're so clever? (*She advances and pinches her.*)

POSVYANTSEVA (*tearing herself away*): Don't touch me!

KAMCHUZHNAYA: You wide-eyed lump! Are you proposing to testify against Kolosovitov?

POSVYANTSEVA: No!

KAMCHUZHNAYA: Are you going to remember Bolosnin?

POSVYANTSEVA: No!

KAMCHUZHNAYA: I'll kill your kid. I'll strangle it myself!

POSVYANTSEVA: I wouldn't put it past you!

KAMCHUZHNAYA: I'll do it! I'll do it! (*Beating her over the head.*)

POSVYANTSEVA (*reeling*): Ah-ah-ah!

KAMCHUZHNAYA: Shut up, you slut! Shut up, you pig! (*She pulls her hair.*)

POSVYANTSEVA (*screams*): Help, help!

KAMCHUZHNAYA (*beating her over the mouth*): Shut up, you rubbish! Shut up!

POSVYANTSEVA (*tearing herself away, rushes to the window, jumps on to the window-sill, breaks the window and holding on to the bars, shouts out*): Save me, save me! They're killing me! Killing me!

Two stalwart Supervisors run in and pull Posvyantseva down from the window-sill. Rublyov, a gloomy looking Colonel with rings under his eyes and grey streaks in his black hair, appears in the doorway.

RUBLYOV: What's going on?

KAMCHUZHNAYA (*trembling in her agitation*): This White Army slut we haven't killed off . . .

POSVYANTSEVA (*her hands and face are covered in blood*): All right! Lock me up! Strangle me! I hate you! You get hold of an unfortunate Russian prisoner of war . . . You get hold of innocent Russian girls . . . (*The Supervisors try to stop her talking.*) You prevent Russian school children! . . . Your hour will come, you executioners!!

Rublyov makes a sign for her to be taken away.

Scene 6

The vast courtyard of a landowner's manor house, which is occupied by Counter-Intelligence SMERSH. To the right we can see the pediment of a large building, the top of which is invisible. There are steps leading up to a wide entrance door. The windows of the first floor are fitted with widely-spaced bars. At the back of the stage we can see an even larger brick building, without any embellishments, the top of which is also invisible, but we can see a semi-basement – it is the same building which was seen from the back in Scene 1. It has been turned into a prison: on its generally dark brown background we can see the windows, which have been freshly bricked up with bright pink bricks all the way up to a small spy hole. To the left of the stage, right across it, there are wrought-iron gates, next to which there is a lodge; it has been turned into a watch tower. There are a couple of flower beds and a defunct fountain. A network of asphalt paths connects various doors of the building on the right with those at the back. By one of the paths, at the crossing of them and almost in the centre, there stands a crude, wooden sentry-box, in which a soldier with colourful little flags directs the traffic; his gestures are elegant, picturesque. All the exits and entrances are at his command. The sentry-box has a loud-speaker. It is a blinding July midday.

The whole scene lasts no more than eight to ten minutes. It is a Pantomime, which consists of constant and tense movements about the yard, the result of the activities of a large and well-ordered establishment.

Along the paths at the back of the stage, guards conduct prisoners from the prison into the building on the right and back again, in particular they lead Pechkurov, Kulybyshev and Klimov back from their interrogation. In order to announce their presence and in order to avoid the possibility of the prisoners meeting each other, the guards click their tongues, clank their keys against the buckles of their belts; they move their prisoners quickly along, putting their charges occasionally into the sentry-box because they must not see each other.

During the time of arrival and departure of prisoners, the traffic-regulating soldier stops the movement of those under investigation. In the course of this scene a couple of small batches of prisoners are brought in and two large ones are being sent off — one, on foot, marches off through the gates, five prisoners to a line, the other by an open lorry, which backs towards the gates; the prisoners sit on the floor of the vehicle, while the guards stand with their backs to the cab.

Among the prisoners there are young women, dressed in West European clothes, as well as Russian peasant women wearing head scarves and carrying bags; young men in soldiers' uniforms and peasants in jerkins; there are many in military great-coats made of Russian cloth, some have white markings 'S.U.' on their backs, but among them there are army uniforms from all over the world. One of the batches of prisoners includes women with children. Some prisoners carry heavy luggage, others have hardly any. The prisoners who are being dispatched emerge from the prison doors, carrying some bread and herring. They talk to each other in a dumb-show, while those who have just arrived are quickly sorted out and taken in. Among those who are about to leave are Yeleshev, Sidorov and Pakhomov.

Numerous Supervisors are rushing around the yard, either attending the prisoners or carrying heaps of files. Sentries come and go, while Sergeants receive or dispatch groups of prisoners.

This silent pantomime is accompanied by the sound of a children's song, which is being rehearsed on radio: it is first performed in toto by a choir, then a solo voice dictates and performs one couplet after another and at the end the whole song is performed again. At the last refrain the curtain comes down.

Happy, victorious
Our country is glorious,
The Kremlin is sparkling with gold.

Stalin, Leader and Guide,
Says we must struggle and fight,
Calls us all to join the fold.

Refrain:
    Our country is happy and free,
    Just look around you and see,
    Don't let it be wasted or sold.

But behind the glorious rainbows
There are enemies lurking about.
We must sweep every one of them out.

    Refrain.

The pantomime is interrupted during this song by distant calls regarding prisoners, as for instance:

SERGEANT: Solovyova!
ANSWER: Oktyabrina, born in 1924 in the town of Hommel, 58-one-A. Ten years.
SERGEANT: Makarova!
ANSWER: Vladilena, born in 1921. Leningrad. 58-one-A. Ten years.
A second time.
SERGEANT: Chugrev!
ANSWER: Ivan. 1918. Village of Lugari, Tambov district. 58-one-B. Ten years.
SERGEANT: Nekurepov!
ANSWER: Gavrila. 1912, village of Merigorye, 58-one-B. Ten years.
He who answers moves over, carrying his belongings from the group which has not been summoned to the group which has.

    Or the pantomime is interrupted by instructions issued by the Duty Officer ('a prayer').
'Attention, prisoners! While you are *en route*, you're not to bend down, not to pick up anything from the ground, not to turn round, not to change places from line to line, not to lag

[79]

behind or get out of line. You are to obey all the orders of
your guards. One step to the right, or one step to the left will
be considered an attempted escape and you'll be shot *without*
warning!'

Or interrupted by his own command:

March, you in front!

*Or by the arrival of the General in his limousine. At this point all
movement ceases. Sentries jump to attention. Supervisors, who
find themselves in his path, salute awkwardly, the ones further
back try to disappear.*

    *Short, fat, pock-marked Colonel Okhreyanov comes dashing
out from the building on the right and arrives just as the tall young
General emerges from his car.*

OKHREYANOV (*making his report*): Comrade Major-General.
During your absence everything's been in order at the Department of Counter-Intelligence SMERSH, which is
under your command!

*The window panes of one of the windows on the second floor of the
building on the right are broken with a loud noise. Posvyantseva
appears in the window.*

POSVYANTSEVA: Help, help! They're killing me, they're
killing me!

*Bolosnin, who is being conducted along one of the paths, jerks his
head upwards and stops still. His guard tries to push him on.
Bolosnin resists, his eyes fixed on the window. Another guard comes
running and the two of them grab his arms and hustle him along.
Posvyantseva is removed from the window.*

GENERAL: How do you work here? (*Wincing.*) Is it always like
that?

OKHREYANOV: Comrade General . . .

GENERAL: No excuses. Investigate and report. There I was in
a good mood, coming here, and all you can do is ruin
everything. Why haven't these flowerbeds been watered?

OKHREYANOV: Comrade Major-General! We water them
every morning and every evening . . .

GENERAL: You call that watered?! The earth's quite dry.

Look. (*He picks up a handful of earth and shows it to him.*) Dry! (*He wipes his hands on a handkerchief and with a wave of his handkerchief dismisses his car.*) Do I really have to look into everything myself? You're to get the heads of departments for a conference with me at 8 o'clock.

OKHREYANOV: Certainly, sir. A conference!

They walk to the building on the right.

After the curtain comes down, the record is obviously stuck and it plays 'Our country is happy and free' at such an unbearable volume that the audience must escape.

Scene 7

A cell. It is day time. A tiny bit of bright sky is visible under the shutter of a spy hole. But the light, on the whole, is grey. There are the same prisoners, with the exception of Yeleshev, Davydov, Wrzesnik and the Prisoner with a black eye. Their 'dinner' is almost over; they have finished drinking the liquid from stew tins and are eating the grain – they have no spoons so that some pour it straight from the tins into their mouths, while others pick it up with their fingers. Halberau is noticeably methodical in his consumption of the grain, which he eats imperturbably to the very end of the scene. The tins, which stand in the places of Mednikov and Bolosnin are untouched, since they are absent.

The curtain has not quite come up yet, but we hear a fierce argument going on, which distracts the prisoners from their precious food. The argument is not just heated, it is painful. Apart from the remarks which we can distinguish, there is a constant hum of 'rhubarb' going on, and which is delivered with great speed.

Rubin is attempting to eat his food automatically, but he has to defend himself from everybody, like a cornered wolf. He is not enjoying his food.

Owing to this argument, Bolosnin's entry is unnoticed. He tries to convey his experiences, but having heard some of the argument, he becomes incensed.

To start with, prisoners are sitting down, but one by one they jump up, and it is only the German and the Italian who remain sitting and observing the Russian argument with consternation.

PECHKUROV: Listen, Rubin, have you ever been to a collective farm?
RUBIN: Yes, I have.

TEMIROV: As a correspondent, no doubt.

KLIMOV (*advancing on Rubin*): So what did you think, tell me, what did you think when the peasants were being destroyed?

RUBIN (*to someone else*): But then we have the underground – the best in the world.

TEMIROV: Nothing but show. Everything's for show. 'The bridges may be made of iron, but their supports are of wood.'

DIVNICH: Yes, I must say, the Soviet people are beggars! When they come to Europe, they're ready to pinch things from the shop counter.

PECHKUROV: What does a collective farmer earn a day? How much per day?

RUBIN: Well, that's because their work is badly organised.

PECHKUROV (*shouting*): Fuck off, you and your organisation! Just give me some land and I'll manage without your organisation.

DIVNICH (*advancing even closer*): Your country is in a state of collapse! It's up the spout! Crazy prices, empty shops! . . .

RUBIN: Well, things were just getting better, when the war got in the way.

KULYBYSHEV: Tell that to the Marines! Ah! War!

KLIMOV: How do you mean, getting better. In 1939 there were thousands of queues for bread all over the country – was that due to war?

GAI: Why did you starve the Ukraine to death? Was that because of the war?

RUBIN: You starved yourselves to death. You left the grain to rot in rubbish dumps.

GAI: We refused to sow it. That's true.

RUBIN: You should have sown it!

GAI: Who for?! Why did you set up a blockade against us? (*He shouts to everyone in the cell*): Quiet, there! Friends! Does anyone know about the blockade of the Ukraine in 1931? When a komsomol would come into your own house and prevent you getting water from your own well! Cattle died off from thirst. My baby sister died!

[83]

DIVNICH: In the twentieth century we have come round to slave labour!

RUBIN: I can't answer you all at once. Let me speak! (*He rushes into the centre of the cell, speaks to them all round, for he is surrounded by enemies.*) Remember what sort of country we had inherited . . .

VOROTYNTSEV: Well, what?

BOLOSNIN (*by the door, furiously*): We should have squashed the bed-bugs first and started the Revolution second!

RUBIN (*twisting and turning in the middle of the cell*): You're all mad! How do you mean 'second'? Human history has lasted ten thousand years and never yet has it seen any justice! Slaves, driven to despair, would rise with Spartacus and Wat Tyler, in copper rebellions or in salt-mine revolts, they would storm the Bastille, there would be Taborite[10] revolts or revolts of the Communes of Muenster and Paris. More often than not they would perish, even before they had had time to rise up from their knees, hardly ever did they manage to get to power and even more rarely did they manage to cling on to it – but never, never did they succeed in embodying the great dream of justice on earth! That is because they had too much trust in yesterday's oppressors, too much charity towards their foes! It was because they took the path of terror and dictatorship with too much doubt and timidity. And so now, when at last, for the first time in many thousands of years, there arose and matured an unconquerable *Science of Revolution*, when an immutable tactic of *Dictatorship* has been evolved, when all the former mistakes of all the previous revolutions have been taken into account, when this tactic has finally succeeded! – when a new world is ready to grow for tens of hundreds of years . . .

DIVNICH: . . . on the bones of a million of . . .

RUBIN: . . . but has had only some miserable twenty-five years . . .

BOLOSNIN: . . . that's half of a human span . . .

RUBIN (*putting one foot on top of the slop bucket*): . . . you un-

[84]

happy, miserable little people, whose petty lives have been
squeezed by the Revolution, all you can do is distort its very
essence, you slander its grand, bright march forward, you
pour slops over the purple vestments of humanity's highest
dreams! There! (*He swiftly sits down on the slop bucket the way
one does and, turning his hands into the lenses of binoculars,
surveys the world around him.*) Here you are! That's your
observatory – this slop bucket! It is from this vantage point
that you observe and learn about the world!

PRYANCHIKOV (*waving someone's torn garment, as if it were a
flag*): Purple vestments, Rubin? Don't make me laugh!

BOLOSNIN (*throws himself at Rubin, but is held back*): While I
was at liberty I did my best to destroy you, you horrors, but
not in order to have to put up with you in a cell!

RUBIN (*jumping up from his slop bucket*): Do you know what you
are – you're Vlasov's lap dog! (*He rushes at Bolosnin, but is also
held back.*)

TEMIROV: These troubadours should be shot: ten years is not
enough!

GAI: Who are the troubadours?

TEMIROV: Any idiot who blows a trumpet is a troubadour!
The hatch is opened. Everybody falls silent, as if cut off.

7TH SUPERVISOR: Anyone with the letter 'K'?

KHOLUDENEV: Kholudenev.

7TH SUPERVISOR: And 'D'?

DIVNICH: Divnich.

7TH SUPERVISOR: Take your things.
*The hatch is closed. Nobody rushes at anybody. Nobody is held
back. There is immobility.*

KHOLUDENEV: M-m-m-yes. The conference continues.
*Both he and Divnich begin collecting their belongings. Everybody
observes them in silence.*

DIVNICH: Even though they give you ten years, there's no
time to argue.

BOLOSNIN (*pouring some tobacco from his own pocket into Divnich's*): You'll get nervous there, have a smoke.

[85]

KHOLUDENEV: Oh dear. We've not had time for a proper chat. Igor! You have such a clear head, what ever brought you back to the Soviet Union? What for? And left your wife behind.

BOLOSNIN: I ask only one thing – don't mention Galina. This question only Mr. Churchill can answer! How I trusted the English! People were warning me, but still I trusted them. It was incredible, it was monstrous, but while they were digging the grave of their own Empire, they disarmed us by deception and gave us up to the Bolsheviks. Hundreds of officers and tens of thousands of soldiers!

VOROTYNTSEV: Mr. Divnich, you were going to tell us what the difference is between the Gestapo and the G.P.U. and you never did.

DIVNICH: Well, it's quite clear that it sounds similar and from the ideological point of view there's no difference at all. In terms of practical application the Gestapo's approach is mediaeval and direct, when they try to find out the truth; they will savagely beat you, torture you, hang you upside down. But if they find that according to their laws you're innocent, they'll let you go, as they let me go. But the N.K.G.B. do not even attempt to find out the truth unless they're trying to unearth some sort of subversive organisation; that's because they're profoundly uninterested in finding out whether you're innocent or not. Whatever happens, you get ten years.

VOROTYNTSEV: Unless they shoot you. Many thanks. It's quite clear.

Divnich and Kholudenev carry their bags towards the door.

BOLOSNIN (*accompanying Kholudenev*): Just think! An extraordinary encounter: they were taking me through the yard, suddenly I heard the window pane breaking and in the window I saw a woman who was clinging to the window bars: 'Help! They are killing me!' And I recognised her as the wife of my war-time friend who got killed. She's a good, charming woman, being tortured right here and you can't do anything to help, and (*gesturing towards Rubin*) there they go trying to prove that it's all within the law.

DIVNICH: Well, friends, since you haven't got a song of your own yet, let's sing one of ours. (*He puts his arms round the shoulders of two of them.*)

(*Several voices sing*):

> Say your prayers, friend, when you're away
> Pray for your country, pray and say:
> Let God protect all those you love
> Let Him protect them from above.

There is a bang on the door and an order to stop the singing. But instead everybody, including Rubin, joins in the song, arms around each other's shoulders and facing the audience.

> Pray to our Lord to give us strength
> To overcome our foes' intents,
> Then peace and love we'll see again
> Above our fields resume their reign.

The door is opened wide with a crash. They all embrace each other in silence. Divnich and Kholudenev leave, the door is shut again, the German continues the methodical eating of his grain. Those who remain embrace each other more closely.

> We are deprived of our land,
> We know we need a helping hand,
> But we believe the time will come
> When we shall win, we'll overcome.

Scene 8

To the left there is a summer pavilion; its façade, with three windows and a porch, faces the audience. The porter is either opening or shutting the door. There is a large notice: RESTAURANT NO. 2, SPECIALITIES. To the right there is an avenue of trees leading away. In front there are two garden benches, one of which is hidden from both the restaurant and the avenue by a semicircle of thick shrubs. There is a lawn in front of the restaurant and in the flowerbed a colourful inscription reads 'Glory to Stalin'. The windows are wide open and by each window there is a small table, while further back there is lively restaurant activity and we can hear cheerful music. Counter-Intelligence Officers walk up and down the avenue entering or leaving the restaurant. There are a few prostitutes. It is a sunny afternoon. As the curtain rises, there is general movement, music, conversation.

Behind one of the windows:

Listen, Miss, I ordered one glass of Château Yquem and one glass of Rhine wine.

I'm sorry.

Well, you should listen carefully.

In the avenue:

Heard about Mymra?

What about him?

He's been appointed Head of the Department.

Okhreyanov seems to like him.

Well, he works with clockwork precision. You should take lessons from Mymra.

Neklyuchimov and Filippov approach.

FILIPPOV: I was trained as an infantryman, became Commander of a machine-gun platoon. I spent almost the entire

war at the front or in hospitals, so I find it rather uncongenial
now to be on prison escort duty; it goes against the grain.

NEKLYUCHIMOV: Yes, Captain, each sort of duty bends you
to its requirements. I don't usually drink, but I would like to
have a drink with you. Let's go.

Behind another window:

We're just routine investigators – donkeys, you might say.
We pull the cart and it's the cart that gets the medals,
wouldn't you agree?

Along the avenue:

That's what Okhreyanov decreed! (*They go past.*)

Comrade Major, is there a political seminar today?

It is Monday, isn't it? No need to ask. At seven. (*They go past.*)

KAPUSTIN (*to Officer No. 3*): Let me tell you about dace. First
of all, it's tasteless, second, it's too dry, third, it's skittish,
while carp . . .

OFFICER NO. 4 (*coming towards them*): Kapustin, lend me
twenty roubles.

KAPUSTIN (*tapping his pockets*): You owe me twenty already.

OFFICER NO. 4: Ten.

KAPUSTIN: Not twenty?

OFFICER NO. 4: No, no. I borrowed and returned it at once.
There was even an I.O.U.

KAPUSTIN (*opening his wallet*): Well, you ought to know; just
before pay day. When will you pay it back?

OFFICER NO. 4: I'll pay it back, don't worry. (*Snatching the
note, he walks quickly away.*)

KAPUSTIN: They snatch half your salary this way . . . Yes, as
to carp . . .

OFFICER NO. 3: Can you lend *me* thirty roubles?

KAPUSTIN: When will you pay it back? (*Gives it to him.*)

OFFICER NO. 3: I'll pay . . . it back . . .

*They enter the restaurant. One of the tables at a window is now
free. Neklyuchimov and Filippov have taken it. Along the avenue:*

TYPIST NO. 1: I know. I've also seen her brother – striped
trousers, wide flares, provincial.

OFFICER NO. 5: What's she like?

TYPIST NO. 1: Well, what do you expect? A plunging neck-line, pink embroidery, got a bow stuck right here, and she struts like a fool.

OFFICER NO. 5: No, I'm talking about her work. She's been sacked, after all; they've opened a file on her ...

TYPIST NO. 1: Oh, I forgot to ask. I never asked. (*They go past.*)

Behind the window:

OFFICER NO. 1: There you go – you live, you breathe, you know nothing, while they compose secret files about you. Each and every year! They can smear you with tar, but if you try to clear yourself ... they never let you see it.

Along the avenue:

NINEL (*clinging to Mymra's arm*): Mymra, you ought to be ashamed of yourself! You've just been promoted and you refuse to treat me.

MYMRA (*as dispassionately as in his investigations*): All right, I'll buy you some pastries.

NINEL: Mymra, that's vulgar. Pastries!

SVERBYOZHNIKOV (*coming towards them*): Comrade Mymra. Congratulations!

OFFICER NO. 6: Comrade Mymra. On your new appoint-ment.

MYMRA: I serve the Soviet Union. Thank you, Comrades. (*They enter the restaurant.*)

TYPIST NO. 2: Goodness, it's hot. Isn't it hot! And look at this trollop, clinging to Mymra already!

TYPIST NO. 3 (*deep voice*): Will they have iced beer, I wonder? (*They enter the restaurant*)

KAMCHUZHNAYA (*to Officer No. 7*): I collect colour photo-graphs. I have a passion for colour photographs.

OFFICER NO. 8 (*to No. 9*): Do you think Okhreyanov has succeeded because of this? (*He points to his head.*) It's because of this. (*He points to the small of his back.*) He began twenty-five years ago as a simple supervisor.

OFFICER NO. 9: Be quiet. Here he is.

Okhreyanov is still out of sight up the avenue, but everybody is already giving way, and, as he approaches, greets him. The last to pass along the avenue are the two Operatives. Kamchuzhnaya comes across them by the porch.

OPERATIVE NO. 1: Hallo, Lydia.

KAMCHUZHNAYA: Hallo, there! Are you free today?

OPERATIVE NO. 1: No, we're on duty.

KAMCHUZHNAYA: What, here?! (*She drags him excitedly onto the bench, which is in the middle of the stage. The 2nd Operative sits down next to them.*) Come on, boys. Who is it? Do tell!

OPERATIVE NO. 1: Why do you have to know? Anyway, you'll see in a minute.

KAMCHUZHNAYA: Come on, Mike. Do tell. I'm one of you. I've never had the chance to do it myself . . .

There is a procession, headed by Okhreyanov and Krivoshchap, which approaches the porch. Okhreyanov moves very slowly; he carries his body as if it were a monument. Some Major, who was coming towards him, is being detained and is apologising about something. The movement along the avenue stops. Those who were behind, having come across this group, wander off; the ones in front return to the restaurant.

FILIPPOV: Why do they call you an astronomer? Are you really an astronomer?

NEKLYUCHIMOV: People can never endure to see someone who's unlike them. I did want to become an astronomer, joined the University of Moscow, but in my second year I was taken away, owing to the Komsomol mobilisation and put into the N.K.V.D. training school. And it was impossible to get away, quite impossible.

OKHREYANOV (*in front of the porch*): Do I really have to examine everything myself? I came here in a good mood, and all you can do is ruin everything. Write me an explanatory memo. (*The Major salutes and leaves rapidly. To the Adjutant*): Do they prune those trees, or not? Where's the Manager?

ADJUTANT: He's away on a job, Colonel.

OKHREYANOV: Issue a reprimand.

ADJUTANT: Yes, sir. (*Making a note.*)

OKHREYANOV (*mollified*): Well, Krivoshchap, since we've got so far, shall we drop in? They say they've got vintage bottles here from the Count's cellar . . .

KRIVOSHCHAP: Let's dive in, sir.

They enter the restaurant. The movement along the avenue resumes. At a window:

OFFICER NO. 1: Who said 'donkeys'? Who said that?

OFFICER NO. 2: (*very drunk*): You . . . s-s-said it! You al-l-lso cr-criticised the f-f-f-iles.

OFFICER NO. 1: Are you off your head? I couldn't have said it. Anya, another bottle, quick!

Along the avenue:

Beef Stroganoff, that's quite something!

I have just sent a typewriter home. Do you think I'll get five thousand for it?

Has it got Russian letters?

No, German.

The adaptation will cost you a cool thousand.

KAMCHUZHNAYA (*indicating the concealed bench*): Over there, all right? (*She walks slowly towards the window.*)

OPERATIVE NO. 2 (*sitting on the bench in the centre*): You shouldn't have told her.

OPERATIVE NO. 1: No matter, the bitch is drunk.

KAMCHUZHNAYA (*from below the window*): Hallo, Astronomer. You're drinking, I see. What's happened?

NEKLYUCHIMOV Captain Kamchuzhnaya, my surname is Neklyuchimov and my first name is Alexander.

KAMCHUZHNAYA (*humming*): Do you remember, Alex, our brief encounters? . . .

NEKLYUCHIMOV: I don't seem to . . .

KAMCHUZHNAYA (*with a break in her voice*): Listen, how can you? . . . How can you? . . . (*She moves away.*)

Along the avenue:

OFFICER NO. 10: I admire the way you work, Comrade

Colonel. You have managed to become an indispensable specialist.

MORGOSLEPOV: My father used to say to me: I'll teach you until it isn't *you* that's looking for work, but *work* that's seeking you out.

OFFICER NO. 11: And how many years did that take? (*They come out towards the porch.*)

MORGOSLEPOV: Seven years at school, six years of factory training, then face-to-face tuition, then correspondence courses. Have you had lunch? I'll go in, my lunch breaks are short. (*He enters the restaurant.*)

OFFICER NO. 10: The bloody hack! But then, even though he managed to displace three Prosecutors, he now works as hard as four.

OFFICER NO. 11: He'll burst from greed, one of these days. He'll even ask five kopecks' change from the waitress. (*He moves away.*)

OFFICER NO. 12 (*nodding after him, to Officer No. 10*): He should talk. He gets twenty packets of cigarettes a month, to soften up prisoners during interrogation, yet he'd sooner choke than part with a cigarette, even though he doesn't smoke. He can't sell them to anyone, so he sends them home in a parcel – his brother smokes. An officer like that should be shot!

FILIPPOV: I saw on a parade ground, with my own eyes, a Sergeant shoot down a couple of Messerschmitts. And now, on my escort duties, who do I see but the very man ...

KAMCHUZHNAYA: Alexander, finish your drink and come here for a minute. I need you.

NEKLYUCHIMOV: This is break time, Lydia. I don't want to talk business.

KAMCHUZHNAYA: Alex, I need you a lot. I wouldn't have asked ...

NEKLYUCHIMOV: Wait for me, Captain, I shan't be long. (*He rises.*)

OFFICER NO. 13 (*walking in front of the flowerbed with Officer*

No. 14): There's one thing I don't understand, George: why did the Americans let us have the Vlasov lot? And the English the Cossacks? What for? What was their aim?

OFFICER NO. 14: D'you want to know what *I* think? Personally? . . . We shall pay for it, by having to fight the Japanese. That'll be our payment, I'm sure of it!

OPERATIVE NO. 1 (*entering the restaurant with No. 2*): In the meantime, Lydia, we'll have a . . . (*Makes a gesture of drinking from a glass.*)

The two Operatives come across Neklyuchimov on the porch.

OPERATIVE NO. 1: Hallo, Astronomer. How are the stars? All in their appointed places?

NEKLYUCHIMOV (*hostile*): Not all of them.

OPERATIVE NO. 2: Some fallen?

NEKLYUCHIMOV: Uh-huh.

OPERATIVE NO. 1: It happens.

They enter the restaurant. Neklyuchimov, following Kamchuzhnaya, walks towards the hidden bench. Kamchuzhnaya sits with her face towards the restaurant, Neklyuchimov with his back to it. There is a slow waltz from the restaurant.

KAMCHUZHNAYA: Alex, did you ever . . . like me . . . a tiny bit?

NEKLYUCHIMOV: Did you call me out for this? . . . (*Attempting to rise.*)

KAMCHUZHNAYA (*restraining him*): It's very important, Alex. Answer me.

NEKLYUCHIMOV: I hate you!

KAMCHUZHNAYA: What for?

NEKLYUCHIMOV: D'you really want to know? A beautiful vase is nothing without . . .

KAMCHUZHNAYA (*triumphant*): So you did . . .

NEKLYUCHIMOV: But I'm married, there's no point in talk like that. Is anything wrong? Are you ill?

KAMCHUZHNAYA: I wouldn't trust your wife if I were you. However, you'll find out about her soon enough. We shan't meet again, Alex.

Scene 8

NEKLYUCHIMOV: Are you going away?

KAMCHUZHNAYA: And yet we might ... meet again ...
Should you need me ... When you're in trouble, in very bad
trouble, just remember, I loved you once! (*She kisses him and
puts her head on his chest.*)
*Operatives No. 1 and No. 2, having left the restaurant, are
walking towards them, but are as yet unobserved by them.*

NEKLYUCHIMOV: What were you about to say?

KAMCHUZHNAYA (*rapidly*): Got anything that should be
destroyed? Addresses? Notes?

NEKLYUCHIMOV: What's the matter?

KAMCHUZHNAYA (*rushing him*): Quickly, my love!

NEKLYUCHIMOV (*hesitating for just a moment; passes his note
book to her*): But why?

KAMCHUZHNAYA (*hiding it*): In your desk? At home?

NEKLYUCHIMOV: Nothing at all. That's the lot.
*Kamchuzhnaya puts her arm round his neck. Almost at once the
Operatives appear from behind the shrubs. Kamchuzhnaya, having noticed them, turns her embrace into a sharp pull with both
hands at his epaulettes. Neklyuchimov jumps up, staring around.
The restaurant music has ceased. The first Operative, stretching
out his arm, shows Neklyuchimov a piece of paper.*

OPERATIVE NO. 1: You're under arrest!

NEKLYUCHIMOV: Me-e?
*He is making an attempt to read the order, but both Operatives are
already rapidly removing his swordbelt, the star from his cap. They
empty his pockets, using all four hands. The second Operative
collects everything and moves on.*

OPERATIVE NO. 1 (*taking out his pistol*): Abo-ut turn! Hands
behind your back! No talking! March!
*There is an upsurge of rumba from the orchestra. They march into
the centre through the thick crowd of Cheka officers, who make way
for them, and they turn right into the avenue: the second Operative
in front, followed by Neklyuchimov, his head bent and his hands
behind his back; the first Operative is behind, his pistol at the
ready.*

[95]

Prisoners

There is a crowd on the porch and people are looking out of the windows, Filippov among them with an expression of horror on his face. Kamchuzhnaya, hidden from everybody by the shrubs, is motionless, pressing Neklyuchimov's epaulettes to her cheeks. The rumba plays on.

Scene 9

A large room, almost a ballroom. There are heavy curtains and electric light. At the back – a rostrum, on which there is a large sculpture of Stalin, full-length, with one arm raised. He is in the uniform of a Generalissimo. On the rostrum there is a table for the judges and the tribunal of Prosecutors; lower down, there is a smaller table for the secretary and lower still a place for the defence counsel and a chair for the defendant. Further downstage there are two rows of dusty chairs, held together by wooden bars, with their backs to the audience. There are two doors, left and right of the rostrum, and another one nearer to us.

As the curtain rises, it is through this door that an usher and a guard conduct Kholudenev, his hands behind his back. They show him his place.

USHER: Arms at the ready!

The guard levels his weapon, the usher leaves. A pause. The guard gradually relaxes his stance. Kholudenev fishes a scrap of paper from his pocket and after some hesitation, shakes tobacco into it.

GUARD: What are you twirling?

KHOLUDENEV: A cigarette, as you can see.

GUARD: What's this paper?

KHOLUDENEV: It's a receipt for my medals and for the watch.

GUARD: How will you get them back then?

KHOLUDENEV: Medals? What do I need them for?

GUARD (*after some thought*): What about the watch?

KHOLUDENEV: It'll get rusty in ten years.

GUARD: I would keep it, all the same. Here's a bit of newspaper.

KHOLUDENEV (*taking the torn-off bit and putting the receipt back into his pocket*): It'll get used – either here or on the way to Siberia, what's the odds?

GUARD: Have some shag. (*Offers him some.*)

KHOLUDENEV: Thanks, if you mean it. (*Pours some into his pocket and adds the rest to his cigarette*) Got a light?

GUARD (*giving him a light*): How many medals?

KHOLUDENEV: I had three.

GUARD: An officer?

KHOLUDENEV: A Captain.

GUARD: What did they arrest you for?

KHOLUDENEV: Well, you see . . .

The same door opens. The guard levels his weapon sharply and moves away from Kholudenev. Kashevarov enters with a bouncing gait. He wears a silk shirt with short sleeves and white trousers. As he approaches Kholudenev he stretches out an accusing hand towards him.

KASHEVAROV: You . . . You there . . . What's your surname? (*Checking in his notebook.*)

KHOLUDENEV (*smoking and leaning back comfortably*): And what sort of employment do you have here?

KASHEVAROV: I'm your State defence counsel.

KHOLUDENEV: Is that so? I rather thought you might be a Captain of the Volleyball Team.

KASHEVAROV: Your surname, what is it?

KHOLUDENEV: Look, why don't you just buzz off; I never engaged you.

KASHEVAROV: True, but the State can't leave you without a defence lawyer.

KHOLUDENEV: That State of yours, as far as I'm concerned can . . . I'd be glad to exchange your State for a chamber pot and top it up.

KASHEVAROV: How do you mean?

KHOLUDENEV: It'd be a damn sight more useful.

KASHEVAROV (*brightening up*): I say, maybe you're not quite all there. Have you had a medical? I could demand that they give you a medical.

Scene 9

KHOLUDENEV (*laughs cheerfully. In a conciliatory manner*): I'll
tell you what, fella-me-lad, I don't get in your way and you
don't get in mine. I'd love to give you a tip, but, alas, I haven't
any cash.

KASHEVAROV: You *are* off your head! You just don't know
the rules. If there's no defence, then there's no prosecution.

KHOLUDENEV: These are excellent rules.

KASHEVAROV: But then how are you to defend yourself? If
you're worried about paying me, it's only some paltry hundred roubles. They'll take them off your receipts.

KHOLUDENEV: What did you say? My receipts? (*Rising*): Get
out of here, you idiot!

KASHEVAROV (*jumping up, in a squeaky voice*): Guard! Aren't
you watching?

KHOLUDENEV: Comrade Guard! Remove him, or I do not
answer for myself.

GUARD (*peaceably*): That'll do. Take it easy.

*A court commandant enters quickly through the right-hand door of
the rostrum. The door remains open and through it we can hear the
voice of Krivoshchap from the neighbouring room: 'The Court
will retire for consultation.'*

COMMANDANT: Everybody rise for the Court!

*Kholudenev has no time to sit down. Krivoshchap, two Assessors,
and a secretary come onto the rostrum. Everybody sits down
simultaneously.*

KRIVOSHCHAP (*rapidly – he is preoccupied*): I pronounce the
session of the military tribunal open. The prisoner will
answer the questions. Your name and surname.

KHOLUDENEV (*gloomily*): Kholudenev.

KRIVOSHCHAP: First name, date of birth?

KHOLUDENEV: All that's been written down a hundred
times.

KRIVOSHCHAP: Are there any objections to the members of
the tribunal?

KHOLUDENEV: That's a matter for the defence. I don't want
any of this.

KRIVOSHCHAP: The rules are immutable. We cannot judge anyone who has no defence. The State allows you to have a fully qualified defence lawyer. Will the two sides take their seats. (*To a clerk*): Proceed.

The defence lawyer, with a sidelong glance at his client, sits down.

KHOLUDENEV (*sitting down*): B-b-bureaucrats ...

1ST ASSESSOR (*mutters rapidly, emphasising occasionally the important, or unimportant passages*): 'I, Major-General and Head of the 2nd Department of Counter-Intelligence SMERSH, Central Army Group affirm ... The indictment was concluded in the case No. 01544/s/31 of Kholudenev, Andrew S. A. S. Kholudenev was arrested and brought to trial by the front-line Counter-Intelligence SMERSH. The investigations have established that Kholudenev, while being an officer of the Red Army, with the last rank of Captain, and a Commander of the Sapper Company, actively conducted subversive, anti-Soviet activity. This subversive activity found its expression, as testified by the Party organiser, U. V. Tyrlykov and the Deputy Political Instructor of the Battalion, G. M. Visgunov, in his allowing the party political and mass educational work to lapse in the subsection entrusted to him (exhibits nos. 25 and 26). In the spring of 1943 Kholudenev called his deputy in the political section, Khukhnobratov, who was the chief political director by the insulting name of "fool" and threatened "to break his legs were he to conduct political discussions at unsuitable times" (exhibits 45, 47, which are Major Khukhnobratov's testimonies). It is in this fashion that Kholudenev has demonstrated his violently terrorist intentions towards the Party's guiding principles. Since the summer of 1943, after the establishment of the deputy commanders in the political sections of companies had been abolished and when the whole of the political activity in his company had become his sole responsibility, Kholudenev, the accused, neglected these duties, announcing in front of his soldiers, even, that the best form of political discussion is "good thick porridge" (exhibit 74). On those rare occasions when he could not evade conducting political discussions, the accused would interpret events in a slanderously untruthful manner and would praise enthusiastically Anglo-American military aid. When, prior to entering German soil, the political section of the division required Kholudenev to give a lecture to the plenary Red Army meeting of the battalion on the subject of "A death for a death, blood for blood", Kholudenev bluntly refused and expressed his beastly anti-Soviet instincts by saying that "Germans are also human" (exhibit 95). One link in the chain of Kholudenev's misdeeds is his close relationship with the chief technician of the same battalion Ivan Novotelov, a survivor of the bourgeoisie, a fierce enemy of progress and of socialism, who escaped the punishment of Soviet Justice by dying on the field of battle. In some of their conversations conducted in a separate tent, but which became known to the members of SMERSH, Kholudenev and Novotelov poured out their hatred towards the great genius the Leader of the Party and of the Soviet people, throwing contempt and insulting nicknames against his shining person, as well as indecent swearing (exhibits 9, 18, 101–103).'

2ND ASSESSOR (*half rising in a pious movement towards the statue of Stalin*): You didn't dare? . . .

KHOLUDENEV: I dared.

1ST ASSESSOR: 'But the accused, together with the deceased Novotelov did not only slander Stalin's brilliant ideas on strategy. In one of their conversations, examining the revolutionary changes in agriculture in 1929–1930 which they interpreted in a criminally incorrect way, they in fact demonstrated that they were defenders of the kulaks and were opposed to complete and voluntary collectivisation. All this gives us grounds for believing that Kholudenev and Novotelov were the instigators of an underground terrorist gang which they failed to form due to the death of one and the arrest of the other. Kholudenev, Andrew, born in 1919, in

the town of Tambov, a Russian, who has no previous record
and is a citizen of the U.S.S.R., a construction engineer by
profession and who served as Commander of a company
with the rank of Captain, who was awarded medals of the 1st
and 2nd category and of the Red Star, is, on the basis of the
aforesaid accused of: conducting base anti-Soviet agitation
together with the deceased co-conspirator Novotelov, was
preparing himself for active subversion and expressed terrorist intentions, i.e. crimes which are covered by articles
58–10–part two, 58–8 to 19 and 58–11 of the Criminal Code of
the Russian Soviet Federal Socialist Republic. Kholudenev
has confessed to the charges and is further convicted by
the testimony of witnesses. According to article 208 of the
Criminal Law Procedure Code, this case is passed on to
Prosecutor Morgoslepov for the accused to be sent for trial.
The indictment is put together by ... signature ... witnessed by ...' (*He sits down and takes a breath.*)

KRIVOSHCHAP: The trial begins. Accused Kholudenev, are
you guilty of the crimes you are accused of?

KHOLUDENEV: What's the difference? Whatever happens ...

KRIVOSHCHAP: In other words, you admit that ...

KHOLUDENEV: Yep.

KRIVOSHCHAP: And you stick to your opinions?

KHOLUDENEV: No.

KRIVOSHCHAP: Is it really true? Have you truly repented?

KHOLUDENEV: Truly, absolutely and finally.

2ND ASSESSOR: Do you really think that the Court will
believe your repentance?

KHOLUDENEV: I don't see why not. Now that I've sorted
myself out, I can see that it wasn't only Stalin, but all of you
and it didn't start in 1929 but in 1917.

Morgoslepov comes running in through the door on the left of the
rostrum. He stands on the rostrum, looking through some papers.

KRIVOSHCHAP: Does the Prosecutor have any questions?

MORGOSLEPOV: No, no, everything is quite clear.

KRIVOSHCHAP: The Defence Counsel?

KASHEVAROV: No.

KRIVOSHCHAP: We will then pass on to the arguments of the two sides. Comrade Morgoslepov, the State Prosecutor has the first word.

MORGOSLEPOV (*very rapidly*): Comrade Judges. Who's this we see before us? We see a man who was nurtured and brought up by our own Soviet country, our own Komsomol. And what do we get by way of gratitude? This degenerate mongrel – I cannot find better words to describe him – took up slandering our wise and brilliant Leader, he did not refrain from open terrorism towards Party leadership and was preparing an armed rebellion . . . ehm-ehm . . . ah . . . preparing to prevent the peaceful conversion of the kulak to socialism. Comrade Judges. There's a limit to our patience. You are the avenging arm of Communist society, of the all-powerful Soviet people. I demand that this accused be given . . . (*he is already on his way out through the same door*) ten years of loss of freedom plus five years without civil rights! (*He has run out.*)

KRIVOSHCHAP: The State Defence Counsel, Comrade Kashevarov, has the word.

KASHEVAROV: Comrades. Being an honest Soviet citizen, a true son of my Socialist Motherland, I've taken perforce the ungrateful duty of defending this bitter enemy, this criminal, who's been so completely exposed. The proof of the accusation is incontrovertible and the Prosecutor could quite rightly have demanded execution for this aggregate of heavy crimes. Comrade Vyshinsky[11] put it so well when he said: 'Everybody's to be shot, like rabid dogs.' In conclusion of my defence speech, I ask that you show clemency to my client and limit his punishment to ten years plus five years without civil rights. (*Exit rapidly.*)

KRIVOSHCHAP: The accused has the last word.

KHOLUDENEV: You can have it.

The usher goes out through the door on the right and we can hear his voice in the next court room, shouting: 'Rise. The Court is coming.'

KRIVOSHCHAP: The Court will retire for a consultation.

They depart. Kholudenev lights up the cigarette he did not finish before the session. A long pause.

GUARD: I must say, Comrade Captain, your remark about porridge is quite true. They feed you on newspaper pulp. (*Pensively*): And what you said about the Germans . . .

The lights go out. They go up again. The second court room is a mirror image of the first. The Prosecutor's rostrum is at the other end. Stalin's statue has the other arm raised. The Court session is in full swing. Divnich is the accused. Kashevarov is the Defence Counsel.

MORGOSLEPOV (*coming to the end of his speech*) . . . Even during the interrogation he had the audacity to explain it as follows (*reading*): 'Spreading the good news is my unavoidable duty, and woe to me if I do not spread the good news.' How do you like that, Comrades? Clear enough, isn't it? Another interesting feature is that he was arrested by the Gestapo and then released. What does that tell us? It tells us that he had found a common language with the Nazi murderers. He will not find such a language with us, Comrades! The accused came back to the Soviet Union with the intention of continuing his subversive anti-Soviet work, hiding behind the banner of progressive religion and even of the latest discoveries in medicine, such as that 'it's not the healthy that are in need of a doctor, but the sick'. Comrade Judges, there is a limit to our patience. You are the avenging arm of the all-powerful Soviet people. I demand that the accused Divnich be given, according to article 58–10 – ten years, according to article 58–4 fifteen years, according to article 58–1A – twenty years, according to article 58–6 twenty-five years imprisonment. In all, then (*to the secretary*) you add it up!

He rushes off towards the left door, being muddled, then remembers

[104]

and turns back towards the right door. Because of his running about, Stalin's statue begins to topple.

KASHEVAROV (*rising immediately at a sign from Krivoshchap*): Comrades, being an honest Soviet citizen, a true son of my Socialist Motherland, I have taken perforce the sad duty . . . *Stalin's statue falls down with a crash.*

DIVNICH (*in an awe-inspiring voice*): Blind leaders of the blind! Who hath warned you to flee from the wrath to come? Verily, verily I say unto you, as the lightning cometh out of the east and shineth even unto the west . . .

Scene 10

A well-appointed drawing room, which has been turned into an office for the Head of Counter-Intelligence. There are Venetian ogival windows and to the right and to the left, oak double doors. A long conference table is covered with a red cloth and at a right angle there is the General's desk. There is a huge portrait of Stalin and a smaller one of Beria.[12] The rest of the furnishings remain as they were in the days of the landowners. Slanting rays of the setting sun come through the windows and shine on the ormolu. The General sits in front, without his uniform jacket, in shirtsleeves, with a Turkish towel over his knees. George, an efficient young batman in a well-fitting uniform without epaulettes, is about to finish the General's toilet and is massaging his neck and cheeks. Colonel Okhreyanov, in a ceremonial uniform with all his medals, stands looking cheerful. He is light on his feet.

GENERAL: D'you know, Colonel, I'm never sick in a 'plane. And wasn't sick today either.

OKHREYANOV: You're very fit, sir.

GENERAL: But then, later, I feel so weak . . . so-o weak . . .

OKHREYANOV: You're overtired.

GENERAL: Well, yes. We spent the whole night, last night, at Beria's. Harder, George, harder.

There is a knock on the door on the left and Rublyov enters. He is gloomy and he stoops.

RUBLYOV: May I? Good evening, Comrade General.

GENERAL: Good evening, Colonel. You look rather grey.

RUBLYOV: I'm ill, Comrade General, I'm very ill.

GENERAL (*carelessly*): As bad as that? Never mind, we'll get you well again. We'll send you for a cure. We must look after the old guard. Incidentally, I'm rather displeased with you.

RUBLYOV: By what, precisely?

GENERAL: Well, listen, this incident today; the Colonel here witnessed it: that shouting all over the yard, the window panes breaking, 'Help, they're killing me.' If you plan to kill, do it in secret, while there are thousands of people in the yard here. What will the guards think? Ours isn't a Nazi torture chamber. It shouldn't be allowed. Kamchuzhnaya, was it? I shall have to punish her.

RUBLYOV: She's a very able investigator. A bit over-enthusiastic, being young. I've looked into it and . . .

GENERAL: For your sake I would have overlooked it, but I'm afraid this time a punishment is due. What was I talking about? . . .

OKHREYANOV: You spent the whole night at Beria's . . .

GENERAL: Yes, at Beria's 'til three in the morning and had to be at the airport by seven . . .

RUBLYOV: Comrade General, permit me to sit down.

GENERAL: You're allowed to sit down, Colonel, do sit down. *Rublyov sits down.*

And just imagine, in the 'plane I was with Sergeyev, Artyom, Voroshilov's adopted son; what's more, he's Svetlana Stalin's friend.

Rublyov is glum, hardly listening.

ADJUTANT (*entering from the left*): Permission to speak, Comrade General. Following your instructions, the members of the conference are now here.

GENERAL: Right. Let them wait. (*Exit the Adjutant.*) He's a splendid fellow, about my age, twenty-four, he's a Major-General, like me, but in the artillery. Not heard of him? He's the one who had that famous contretemps with Rokossovsky.

OKHREYANOV: I don't quite recollect, Comrade General . . .

GENERAL: Well now, that's something you must know about, how he paid Rokossovsky back – the whole of the First Byelorussian front line were killing themselves laughing. In Moscow they appointed Artyom Commander of the artillery brigade. However, its tractors were not much good, so, through Voroshilov, he managed to get a completely new set of tractors, which were being transported by train. Artyom arrived ahead at the headquarters of the front. And suddenly he's told that it's not he but some old fogey who's been appointed. Right! He phones Moscow, Moscow phones Rokossovsky, who says, would you believe, that he regrets, but the appointment cannot be changed: it's been signed. (*His toilet is finished.*) 'Is that so?!' He issues an order: the train turns back. So the tractors left for Moscow, away from the battle front. I tell you, they all roared with laughter at the Byelorussian front.

OKHREYANOV (*laughing*): The train turned back. Wonderful.

GENERAL: But what do you think of Rokossovsky! He might be sorry! The shit! Has he forgotten . . . George, you can go. (*George collects the toilet articles and loiters.*) Has he forgotten the two occasions in 1938 when he was taken out into the forest to be shot, to put the fear of God into him? Incidentally, Lavrentiy Beria said something – it's for your ears only – (*exit George rapidly through the door on the right*) – 'If necessary, we'll take him out for the third time and won't bring him back; we must end these Zhukov habits!'

OKHREYANOV: End these Zhukov habits! That's right. These Generals have been getting out of hand.

GENERAL: The Cossack host! These Partisans! . . . Yes. Only, I must admit that at that point the battle front was still at the Dniepr, so the whole thing is a bit of a fiction. All right, Colonel. You can call them in. (*Exit right.*) *Okhreyanov walks round to the back of the General's desk and rings.*

ADJUTANT (*entering*): Yes, Comrade Colonel.

OKHREYANOV (*his demeanour completely changed. He is taller, there is something steely in his immobility*): Let them . . . ehm . . . come . . . *The Adjutant salutes and exit. Okhreyanov, indicating a place of honour.*

OKHREYANOV: Change your place, Prokhor.

RUBLYOV (*sitting half-turned in a low armchair in front of the conference table*): I'm all right here.

Okhreyanov sits down at the side of the General's desk. Members of the conference begin coming in from the left. They behave quietly. There are more than twenty of them, from the rank of Major upwards. Among them – Morgoslepov, Krivoshchap, Sophia Lvova, a tall, grey-haired medical officer, Ognida, Kapustin and others. There is some awkward clearing of throats, a low hum of conversation. They settle down around the table and on divans along the walls.

OKHREYANOV: Kapustin, why haven't you finished announcing the decrees of the Special Conference?

KAPUSTIN: I thought, Colonel . . . It was physically impossible.

OKHREYANOV: We've just locked up an astronomer, now there's a physicist here. (*Laughter.*) It's best not to think. A turkey died of thinking. (*He walks towards the door on the right. As he approaches it he begins to tiptoe. Peeps through it, then jumps away.*) Attention!

Everybody rises. The General enters.

GENERAL: All right. You may sit down.

Everybody sits. The General walks briskly towards his desk and, still standing, sorts out his papers. There is a deathly hush. Okhreyanov also sits down, having moved his chair completely silently.

GENERAL: So . . . I've gathered you here, Comrades, I've gathered all of you who are in charge of those who work in our Counter-Intelligence, so as to outline most clearly, most precisely the basic problems facing us today. I have just returned from a Conference of the heads of the front line departments of SMERSH, as well as of the regional management of the N.K.G.B., which lasted three days and was under the chairmanship of Lavrentiy Beria. Yesterday it had the greatest honour and happiness of being visited personally by Comrade Stalin!

General applause, everybody rises, Rublyov with difficulty. He is the first to sit down again.

GENERAL: Comrades! I will not speak of that enormous excitement, which took hold of me, when I saw the face so familiar and so dear to us all, the face of the greatest friend to Counter-Intelligence, of the fighter for the peace of the whole world, of our great Father, Friend, Mentor and Leader. Comrades, Comrade Stalin greatly appreciates the efforts of our Organs in defence of our country during the war. I shall repeat verbatim truly historic words, which were uttered yesterday by Comrade Stalin. He said: 'It is now clear that without the Cheka we wouldn't have won the Civil War and without the N.K.V.D. we would not have won the Great Patriotic War.' But, Comrades, is it typical of Bolsheviks to rest on their laurels? No, a hundred times no! The greatest danger now, is that we, the Cheka Officers, might relax, and say the war is over and we can slow down, etc. Yesterday, Joseph Vissarionovich made a joke. He said: 'Your troops, Lavrentiy, spend the whole of the war in the Third Echelon and now want to push forward to the front'. That is something we, each and every one of us, must understand and see where it is meant to lead us.

RUBLYOV: Comrade General, allow me to leave.

GENERAL: What's that? No. The war may be finished for the Army, but for us now it is the battle for Stalingrad, the major combat, the very peak of fighting. And our struggle is uneven, Comrades, numerically speaking. Our SMERSH management could be compared, say, to a select battalion of officers (without counting supervisory staff or the escort armies) who have to grind down whole divisions of the enemy – just look: they crowd our prison yards in whole divisions – do not count them as your compatriots, forget that they are Russians – they are a bitter, degenerate rabble who have breathed the poisoned air of Capitalist Europe. Today our responsibility is great. We, the Cheka officers, must be especially merciless, especially severe, so as to be

able to fulfil the task of repatriation which has been entrusted to us by great Stalin. Read and re-read, Comrades,
the amnesty which was published yesterday and which
marks the fruits of our glorious Victory. Each and every one
who deserted is forgiven by the Soviet government. Why is it
so, Comrades? Because a deserter is nothing but a coward,
he wants to save his own skin, but he is one of us, he is
socially close to us, Comrades. But he who was not afraid of
being in the front line, not afraid of dive bombers, not afraid
of 'Tigers', will not be afraid of turning the gun against us,
and so forth. These decisive days what do we see among us,
Comrades? On the one hand we record, we put up a roll of
honour to our best workers: the President of our military
tribunal Krivoshchap, our prosecutor Lieutenant-Colonel
Morgoslepov, Major Ognida, Captain Mymra and so on and
so forth. But, Comrades, we cannot and we must not cover
up our deficiencies. I don't even want to mention that
shameful case where we overlooked in our own ranks that
double imperialist agent, the bourgeois degenerate Neklyuchimov. The responsibility for that lies on all our collective shoulders, but in the first instance, the responsibility is
yours, Comrade Rublyov and yours, Comrade Okhreyanov.
Let this be a lesson to you; the steely arm of the Cheka knows
how mercilessly to eradicate even in its own back yard. But,
Comrades, Comrade Stalin gave us a directive of genius,
that our methods of investigation are still too liberal, that
they are still in the rotten grip of juris*prun*dence and that
using methods like these we will never solve the problems of
today, of that enormous human flood which pours into this
country from the West; we will never solve it on time. As
always, Comrade Stalin has dialectically extracted the most
important link of the chain, when he said all this must come
to a stop. It's time to stop it, Comrades! Just examine the
methods of our best front-runners, those of Comrade Krivoshchap or of Morgoslepov. It's harder for them, don't you
think? There is a whole crowd of you interrogators, while

they are on their own and they are pressurised by various social norms and forms; they, indeed, could have become the bottleneck, but they have managed not to. Being men of high social conscience, they know how to organise their work so as to double, quadruple the effectiveness of the Tribunal's output. It wasn't long ago that we considered convicting forty people a day the maximum we could manage and now we're convicting a hundred and twenty and – the more the merrier. What, in principle, is new about it? First, as a result of Comrade Krivoshchap's initiative, we've got rid of the so-called 'discussion' room – and cigarette smoking now takes place after work. In the first room, now, we listen to the evidence, and we sentence in the second, then in the first room we sentence and in the second we listen to the evidence. Also, the sentencing department's work is very precise and meticulously prepares all the sentences no later than the day before the trial. Finally, owing to Comrade Morgoslepov's initiative, we have a flow system which enables us to have both sessions of the Tribunal serviced simultaneously. The question is why such brave innovatory methods, which have been borrowed from industry, are not initiated among the investigators?

RUBLYOV: (*rising. It has been obvious throughout that he has been in great pain*): I . . . must go . . . (*He walks towards the exit.*)

GENERAL (*looking him up and down, very perplexed*): . . . Whose fault is it that the investigators are trailing behind? It's the fault of the heads of department, yes!

Rublyov, before reaching the door, sinks onto the parquet floor. Confusion.

VOICES: What's wrong with him?

Sophia!

Why don't you lift him up?

Take him to the clinic!

Who's on duty there?

The doors are flung open. A couple of Lieutenants and a couple of Sergeants carry Rublyov awkwardly out. Sophia Lvova leaves

*behind them. The members of the conference settle down again. We
can still hear:*

He's had it for a long time . . .

Cancer of the liver, or something.

I, too, have a terrible pain here . . .

GENERAL: Yes . . . Poor old thing's going down . . . Burnt
himself out, working for the Cheka. I shall continue. It's you,
you who are in charge of the workers, you've allowed this
relaxed attitude, it's you who do not control the speed of
investigations, it's you who allow the investigations to drag
out for a month or more. That's quite insupportable! Your
interrogators loll about in their armchairs as if they were at
the barber's. Colonel Okhreyanov, you're to exchange them
for hard chairs . . .

OKHREYANOV: . . . Yes, sir. Exchange for hard chairs.
(*Makes a note with zeal.*)

GENERAL: . . . What is it that they twitter about with the
prisoners, I'd like to know? Indeed, as I walk along the
corridor – is there a raised voice, or a female scream? There
isn't even a swear word, as if you're walking in a sanatorium
and not Counter-Intelligence SMERSH. Last month I received only seventy-one notifications of increased physical
pressure, which makes only one and a half per cent of all the
cases investigated – what about the rest ? Do they manage
without? But where are the results? How many cases are
being dealt with in one week? All of them must be finished!
Our motto is: he who is arrested on Monday is to be tried on
Saturday – that's all there is to it. (*Drinks some water.*) Also –
I'm sorry Sophia Lvova has left – the health clinic gets in
the way: out of seventy-one notifications three were objected
to on the grounds, if you please, of the extreme physical
weakness of the accused, so that I had to issue a second
approval. This holds things up, after all! It's no accident that
owing to flabby and badly organised evidence the Tribunal is
unable to bring out a verdict. As for the Special Conference
Decree, the Tribunal comes up with an eight year sentence

and even, in some cases – I was ashamed in front of Beria – a five year one. Where are we going, Comrades?! No, we must abandon this rotten practice. You're not making use of that brilliant advanced technology which the Soviet Government has provided for you. For instance, what prison cells are you making use of? You make use of ordinary ones, with wooden floors – grandfather's technology, early nineteenth century. Colonel Okhreyanov, you're to pull up the floor boards.

OKHREYANOV: ... Yes, sir. Pull up the floor boards! (*Makes a note with zeal.*)

GENERAL: The majority, of course, are placed in damp ones with cement floors – that's all right as far as it goes. But I've brought with me permission to set up ten standing cells. A man is squeezed in by the door closing and there he is. If he tries to sit down, he's left hanging by his back and bent knees. Despair, of course; he can't tell if he's walled in for ever ... You could even summon a plasterer and start a discussion in the corridor about plastering the door in ... It is only for four hours in twenty-four that they push a rod through for him to lean on. It's a very ingenious construction. I've brought sample designs with me to show you. Apart from all this, for the most obstinate categories, I've Comrade Beria's permission to make use of the old and well-tried method of putting pressure on the genitals! (*Applause.*) That's the kind of lever which can ... well, I don't know! While we spend our time force-feeding through a tube! ...

Scene 11

A sumptuous, gloomy study. On the back wall there is a large map of Europe on which a red thread indicates the 1945 demarcation line. There is a large portrait of Stalin. All the curtains are drawn. There is a large antique desk and another one at right angles to it. Close to the door there is a small bare table for the accused, and a stool. The middle of the study is almost empty. The room is in half-darkness. Rublyov is lying down on a couch. He half rises with an agonised groan and lowers his feet. He is dressed. Sophia Lvova enters without knocking. She wears an overall on top of her uniform.

SOPHIA: Colonel Rublyov, lie down. We'll give you another injection in a minute.

RUBLYOV: Lieutenant-Colonel, stop pretending that you're a sister of mercy. You're nothing but an old prison doctor.

SOPHIA: A doctor's always a doctor.

RUBLYOV: Not always in a prison. You cannot help me, you cannot save me, so let me die in peace. (*Sophia takes his pulse.*) What are you doing? I have no pulse, didn't you know? (*Pulls his hand away.*)

SOPHIA: You have, but it's very weak.

RUBLYOV: I'm one of those who hasn't got one. I quite simply haven't got one! All that's invented for idiots.

SOPHIA (*anxiously*): You should be lying down. Drink this. There'll be a 'plane tonight and we'll send you to a Berlin clinic.

RUBLYOV: Why not to a Moscow one? Have the Germans got all the answers? (*He drinks his medicine.*) Tell me, why are the healthy so afraid of the dying? Why do they lie? It's an hour

[115]

since you said: a few days of suffering and then death for sure. You said it, didn't you?

SOPHIA: Wh-who did I say it to?

RUBLYOV: You've been working in these departments for years – and you ask – to whom? In front of whom? All right, when the aeroplane comes, give me a ring. (*He dials a number on his own telephone.*) Get Vorotyntsev here from one hundred and twenty-five.

SOPHIA: Colonel Rublyov, after such an attack . . . (*as if trying to prevent him telephoning.*)
A knock.

KAMCHUZHNAYA (*in the doorway*): May I come in, Comrade Colonel?

SOPHIA: Captain Kamchuzhnaya, Colonel Rublyov is ill and can't see anybody.

KAMCHUZHNAYA: Excuse me . . . (*To Rublyov*): You said at nine, but if you're ill . . .

RUBLYOV: Come in.
Kamchuzhnaya enters. Sophia shrugs her shoulders and leaves.

KAMCHUZHNAYA: Comrade Colonel, I have two small questions. The accused Rubin . . .

RUBLYOV: Well?

KAMCHUZHNAYA: According to the reports from cell 117 where he was held earlier, as well as now from 125, he conducts himself in the cell arguments as a true loyal Marxist, defending the Soviet Regime as well as the organs of Security, although not with regard to himself. During the investigations he continues to insist that the case was cooked up against him and is due to a squabble in the Army political section. This seems to me to be correct. The Divisional Commander heard of Rubin's arrest and sent a splendid character reference, which contradicts the one from the Political Section. We've also received, apart from that, references about his military conduct from officers who are members of the Party and who fought with him.

RUBLYOV: It's to be included in the surveillance file.

KAMCHUZHNAYA: Who, the officers? I've done that as a matter of course.

RUBLYOV: The Divisional Commander as well.

KAMCHUZHNAYA (*surprised*): The Divisional Commander as well?

RUBLYOV: The motto is: the days of Zhukov are over.

KAMCHUZHNAYA: Ye-es. I un-der-stand. But I was talking about Rubin. He is sincerely devoted to the idea of Communism, he has two medals, been wounded twice . . .

RUBLYOV: So what?

KAMCHUZHNAYA: I understand, of course, that he can't be freed, you'd need the Minister's approval . . . But suppose he was freed on condition he works for us . . . as an informer? To deal with delicate matters to do with ideology. He's an educated person, used to teach Marxism-Leninism – which is important. Students after the war . . .

RUBLYOV: He's too complicated. He'll never become an informer. What are you so worried about? Who's the other one?

KAMCHUZHNAYA: Professor Mostovshchikov. Our scientific experts have confirmed that he's an outstanding specialist in atomic physics. In Europe he worked in . . .

RUBLYOV: Be brief.

KAMCHUZHNAYA: Maybe he shouldn't be in the general flow. A person like that might be needed, and probably soon.

RUBLYOV (*speaking with difficulty and some pauses*): 'Soon'-nothing. He's to be in the general flow! In fact, I instruct you to see to it that he's sent off on a special Polar detachment intended for particularly heavy physical labour. Of course, we'll see to it that he doesn't die. When he gets to a certain point, he'll be yanked out, sent to Lubyanka; some respectable General would express his sincere regrets about not having known in time that such a great scientist was in need of help and defence and would respectfully *beg* the Professor to return to his scientific studies, but to overlook the inconvenience of the barbed wire around his laboratory.

Mostovshchikov, who until recently had been beaten over the head by some miserable guard, would experience bliss, a renewal, and not to have to pick-axe the frozen soil of Siberia for an inch of butter for his breakfast, he would do more for us than for all the tea in China.

KAMCHUZHNAYA (*overwhelmed*): What a profound thought!

RUBLYOV: We've had some experience. Systems similar to this have been in operation for some fifteen years and with great success. That's how the best machines in our Air Force were made. You know, Kamchuzhnaya, that we're not rich, we have few resources. Instead of which we have to study the human psyche. Is that all?

KAMCHUZHNAYA: Yes, sir.

RUBLYOV (*approaching her*): Let me tell you something, Lydia. (*He puts his hand on the nape of her neck.*) You could have become a good investigator, a high flyer, but you take it too much to heart. You're too enthusiastic.

KAMCHUZHNAYA: Is that . . . a bad thing?

RUBLYOV: Nobody needs it any more. It was needed some time ago, long ago, when the wheel was being run in. It runs now, and all you have to do is give it a drop of oil. Keep your heart to yourself. This thing today, with the window being broken. I was trying to promote you to head of the department, but now Mymra's been appointed. Mymra would never let things get so public but all his papers would be duly signed. Why don't you become a Mymra? Or else leave the department altogether, eh?

KAMCHUZHNAYA: But I don't want to become a Mymra!

RUBLYOV: Then leave. You can't be all that fond of this work. I can't remember how you joined . . . Ah, yes. Through your husband. To whom you said: first, tell me all about it; then, let me come to the interrogation (I'll be behind the curtain), then you joined the courses . . .

KAMCHUZHNAYA (*with fervour*): Colonel. This is my kind of work. I've a talent for it – I understand people, I guess things quickly, I remember things . . . And you tell me to give it up

... (*With compassion*): What's wrong? You've never talked to me ... You've always been ... I'm afraid to come close to you.

RUBLYOV (*thinking his own thoughts*): Drop it, Lydia ... Drop it and run ...

KAMCHUZHNAYA: It so happens, I'm in terrible trouble to-day. May I tell you? ...

GUARD (*peeping through*): Comrade Colonel, excuse me.

RUBLYOV: Yes, yes.

Vorotyntsev enters; his hands are behind his back but he frees them as he comes into the study. Rublyov dismisses the guard with a nod. Kamchuzhnaya, annoyed, walks past Vorotyntsev, looking him up and down. She leaves.

RUBLYOV: Well, Mr. Vorotyntsev, how are you? (*He switches on the ceiling light.*)

VOROTYNTSEV: Better than you'd wish.

RUBLYOV: You didn't expect to be summoned?

VOROTYNTSEV: I did sign article 206, what else is needed?

RUBLYOV: The thing is ... you know ... in my private capac-ity ... I wanted to let you know that your case is to be heard by the military tribunal – tomorrow.

VOROTYNTSEV: Did you have to take the trouble just for that?

RUBLYOV: Apart from that ... *He suffers a sharp attack of pain. He stumbles backwards, his head thrown back, across the middle of the room. He knocks against an armchair and sits down in it. Controlling himself*) Apart from that, I wanted to warn you about your fate ...

VOROTYNTSEV: It was decided before the trial. I understand that. As in every other case ...

RUBLYOV: Decided, yes, but differently from all the others.

VOROTYNTSEV: I understand that too. I shall be shot.

RUBLYOV (*looks at him fixedly*): You're mistaken. You'll be hanged.

VOROTYNTSEV: And, of course, secretly. In a corner.

RUBLYOV: The day after tomorrow.

VOROTYNTSEV: I've worked that out. Is that all?

RUBLYOV: What else do you want?

VOROTYNTSEV: There's nothing else that I can expect from a Bolshevik Government. I know, it's the end. May I go?

RUBLYOV: Don't tell me you're more comfortable there than here? The air is fresh here, there are comfortable armchairs here, instead of straw, slop buckets, stench.

VOROTYNTSEV: People are clean there.

RUBLYOV: Wait and you'll understand why I summoned you. Do sit down. No, not there – on the couch.

Vorotyntsev, however, sits down by the empty table for the accused. Rublyov moves towards him, dragging his chair right up to the little table and sits down.

RUBLYOV: Tell me, Colonel, how come you have such bright eyes? Your back is so straight – why? You hold your head up high – why? You've known for a long time that we would execute you, after all. You are going to die, die the day after tomorrow! Have you no fear of losing your life, tell me, Colonel? Maybe you have some secret . . . you know something? (*They stare at each other.*) I don't ask out of sheer curiosity. I'm also a condemned man. There's no salvation for me either. I have a terrible illness. Today is the 9th of July. By the 15th I'll no longer be here. Forget who I am. Today I'm no longer your enemy. I summoned you out of friendly feelings. Because now you're no longer an enemy of mine.

VOROTYNTSEV: I wish you *were* an enemy. As the saying goes, I respect courage even in a Tartar. But you're not an enemy. You're an executioner.

RUBLYOV: But your side – did you have no executioners? *Will* you not have any?

VOROTYNTSEV: Not the same quantity. Not the same quality.

RUBLYOV: Each party maintains three executioners for each 'troubadour'. How can you have a political party without executioners?

VOROTYNTSEV: We're not a party. Fortunately, or unfortunately, we never were a party. Otherwise, we might have won.

RUBLYOV: Lying on the couch just now in a cold sweat, in pain, I understood that I'm as lonely as a wolf; that *they* needed me while I held them together; while I pushed them on; but now that I'm a burden, they are in a hurry to get rid of me; they've found a replacement ... And so I thought of you with gladness, of someone who's going the same way ... Forget that I'm a Colonel in the N.K.G.B. In a few days these distinctions between us will disappear. So – man to man, a traveller to another traveller, can you help me?

VOROTYNTSEV: To be quite honest, having emerged from a cell and just one day from being hanged, I find it difficult to want to help you.

RUBLYOV: I understand, I know! But can't you rise above it? I've never been a coward, but I'm so frightened now. I used to be flint hard, so why am I crumbling now? I want to meet death with the same defiance shining in my eyes as in yours. Teach me the secret of your fortitude.

VOROTYNTSEV: There's no secret. I'm already 69 years old and I can see that I've followed the right path. Why should I lose courage?

RUBLYOV: How do you mean, the right path? What right path? You're a professional soldier. How many wars did you take part in?

VOROTYNTSEV: Five.

RUBLYOV: The Russo-Japanese? Which you lost. The Russo-German? You lost that too.

VOROTYNTSEV: We didn't lose it. It was because of you.

RUBLYOV: The Civil War? Lost again. The Second World War? Beaten again.

VOROTYNTSEV: You left out the Spanish Civil War.

RUBLYOV: For twenty-eight years we've been beating you in everything, and everywhere and today we've finally crushed you – and you say you have no reason to lose courage? The whole of your life is a road of utter defeat – and you consider it the right path?

VOROTYNTSEV: It was right, in the sense that I didn't make a mistake about whose side to be on. I always took the right side – *against you.* I never wavered, I never doubted, I never thought that truth was on your side. I never thought of joining you. However many your triumphs, I was always against you . . . One thing was certain: never to allow, never even to surmise that some tiny part of the truth was on your side – that was right! Yes, we've failed. But you haven't won either. That's why my eyes are bright. I've lived long enough to see that you haven't won either! That's why!

RUBLYOV: Today? You say that today. Are you quite sober?

VOROTYNTSEV: Yes, today, in the hour of your greatest outward victory, even in your prison and before my very death I've been given to see that you have lost utterly! That you're doomed! You persecuted our Monarchy, and look at the filth you established instead. You promised paradise on earth, and gave us Counter-Intelligence. What is especially cheering is that the more your ideas degenerate, the more obviously all your ideology collapses, the more hysterically you cling to it. That means you're finished. Without this pathetic ideology of yours you might have saved yourselves. With it – it's all up with you. For the last twenty-eight years Russia has never been quite so far from Bolshevism. In the Counter-Intelligence cell I saw it quite clearly – Russia does not belong to you, Comrades! The people in that cell are different from the ones you arrested in 1918. They do not wear signet rings on their white fingers, their forage caps still bear the marks of the five-cornered star. They're all young, brought up in *your* schools, not ours, on your books, not ours, in your faith, not ours – but they've grown up . . .

RUBLYOV (*nodding*): Not ours, but not yours either.

VOROTYNTSEV: A tiny whiff of freedom was enough to blow away the black cloud of your magic from the youth of Russia! You used to revile the first wave of émigrés, you said that they were mercenary; that they didn't want to understand progressive ideas. Maybe so. But where does this *second* wave of émigrés come from – all those millions of simple Russian lads who have tasted twenty-four years of a new society and refuse to return home?

RUBLYOV: How do you mean, refuse? Where did you come across them? In the cells? They came back, quite voluntarily. They are coming back – that's the surprising thing! But they'll be sent into camps – and your second wave of émigrés will vanish!

VOROTYNTSEV: But then, how come they didn't understand your progressive ideas? As far as I can see, they reject your ideologists.

RUBLYOV: They reject your saints as well. They don't need our ideas – they have their own: to do a bit of moon-lighting, to pinch what is available, to spend it all on drink, to have it off with a skirt.

VOROTYNTSEV: Natural demands, after all. What they want is to live, let's face it.

RUBLYOV: Now, that's sensible. We agree at last . . . You, on the other hand . . .

VOROTYNTSEV: But you prevent them living.

RUBLYOV: You, on the other hand, suffer from some kind of naïve illusions. We prevent them living? How, then, do you explain the way we've taken off? You must look at facts, Colonel. The fact is, that Marxism has not yet reached its centenary, but look at the size of the continent we've acquired. (*He indicates the map.*) And we're still growing. (*He is exhausted and sits down.*)

VOROTYNTSEV: Yes, I must say, there have been years when one could have lost courage. I've been defeated many times – however hard one worked, however hard one tried – it all vanished without trace. It seemed that even when no mistakes were made, there was one defeat after another. Why? I don't know. There seems to be some divine and limitless plan for Russia which unfolds itself slowly while our lives are so brief. There are moments when at some event one is even seized with mystical terror – and even asks oneself: why is everything so useless?! But don't keep on referring to your victories. Looking back, one can explain away each one of them, crack it open like a walnut. The Civil War? (*He rises and thereafter he paces about the room.*) Imagine you're an English Minister in 1917 and look at Russia from there. What a country! An ocean of pearly grain. Ancient, solid forests, the size of several Europes! The bowels of the earth bursting with whatever a human being needs on this planet. Hundreds of navigable rivers, swarming with fish and flowing into oceans, warm or cold, fresh water or salty. Within some paltry twenty years we developed oil fields, quarries, coal mines, factories, railways. Within some paltry ten years we had Stolypin[13] villages everywhere. Were you to give them liberty, we could have had a second America of prosperous farmers. Siberia, that frightening, impenetrable Siberia, the haunt of bears and vagrants, was on the point of becoming another Canada – four times as vast . . .

RUBLYOV: Don't go too far! Illusions again! And don't you steal *our* achievements!

VOROTYNTSEV: But what have you done to Siberia? Instead of filling in the marshes with wooden logs, you've filled them in with corpses. Along the wastes of the Yenisey river you put up barbed wire. Along the Arctic Ocean you've put up the fences and observation towers of the labour camps. One of your most arrogant myths is that you have developed Russian economy. But what you've done is to cripple its original thrust. A factory is in the wrong place, approaches to it are from the wrong end, any new building needs repairs within three months. I've been watching you all these years with all the attention of hatred and I haven't missed a thing!

RUBLYOV: Magnitogorsk. Turksib – I'm too lazy to enumerate them all. Kuzbassk for coal . . .

VOROTYNTSEV: But the twentieth century is not set in concrete . . .

RUBLYOV: Balkhashsk for copper smelting . . .

VOROTYNTSEV: While the copper itself is a thousand miles away. Just tell me, do you think that without you there would have been no radio broadcasts, no electrified railways? Don't pretend that progress is because of your system. You're trailing behind the century and when you have to fight, the trouble is you don't know which way to turn and you foul it up . . . The Russian people used to be hardworking . . .

RUBLYOV: . . . for the landowners . . .

VOROTYNTSEV: . . . good-natured . . .

RUBLYOV: . . . in front of the police . . .

VOROTYNTSEV: . . . adaptable, many-sided, exceptionally gifted . . .

RUBLYOV: . . . but not allowed to go to school . . .

VOROTYNTSEV: That's another myth. As to you, what sort of people did you condemn on political grounds? Read your own trumped-up cases. Every one of them was at the bottom of the heap. A nation, which was only just beginning to become aware of itself, the immense powers of which were still unfathomed, a nation of 170 million, whose soldiers held up the Eastern Front of Europe . . .

RUBLYOV: . . . but lacking ammunition . . .

VOROTYNTSEV: They had ammunition! That's another myth! I was in the trenches, I know. By 1917 we were armed to the level of Verdun. Suppose there had been a revolution in America in 1941 – you could have said with assurance that they 'had no Air Force' – but they built it during the war!

RUBLYOV: So where were your arms?

VOROTYNTSEV: At the front! But it was you who gave them away to the Germans after the peace treaty of Brest. They were also in the rear, but for three years you used them against us and later used them to train your Army . . . That this nation could give up the Straits to that nation, to the Germans. So as to have to face their fleet in the Mediterranean? For a hundred years, seven generations of English politicians, twenty-five government administrations spent

[125]

their time digging, delving and building so as not to let the Germans through, and you caved in. England fought against Germany, but was equally afraid of Russia. But then suddenly there emerged a handful of unknown rogues from among 'professional revolutionaries', that's to say, from among those who chose destruction as their profession, who had never in their lives created anything, who were incapable of creating anything, people who belonged to no nation, who had no experience of practical life, irresponsible chatterers, who spent half their lives in third-rate cafés ...

RUBLYOV: That's what's known as self-criticism. Did you reconstruct this from your experience of White émigrés?

VOROTYNTSEV: To some extent, yes ... And it was that handful of rogues that managed to decompose an Army ten million strong, to take an unarmed Petrograd with the bayonets of drunken sailors – so that the fields were left unsown, factories grew silent, the mines were left to silt up and Russians began to destroy Russians, breaking their lances, not over Constantinople, but over Novocherkassk. Tell me, sir, you English Minister, do you like this Communist Party? Don't you think this kind of Party suits you well? Don't you think this sort of Party is quite exceptional? No Lawrence of Arabia, no British Intelligence Service could have invented a better one. There was no need to strangle it. (*Pause.*)

RUBLYOV: Well, from the English point of view ...

VOROTYNTSEV: From the French point of view as well ... It's that that saved you. It wasn't Marti or the International Proletariat. 'Intervention', 'the campaign of fourteen states' – all rubbish. Two companies in Odessa, a battalion in Archangel and disembarcation in the Far East, but without any further movement – none of them fought, there was no 'campaign of the fourteen', only Poland! Just remember, from your first appearance, nobody abroad feared you or took you seriously, considering – unfortunately without foundation – that your whole enterprise was a circus.

RUBLYOV: What, even Hitler? Did he think it was a circus when he had to retreat? Was he having fun when he surrendered Berlin?

VOROTYNTSEV: Even Hitler – he more than anyone. Mistake upon mistake. But what have you to be proud of in your war with Hitler? A devastated country? The blockade of Petrograd? Some fifteen million killed? Drowning in blood and boasting of victory! Haven't you been proclaiming for twenty-four years that you wouldn't let anyone pass; that you could resist any alliance, that you would fight on someone else's territory, that you would shed hardly any blood, while Hitler, all on his own, beat you as he pleased, where he pleased, with lunch-breaks and rest days on Sundays. *We* didn't retreat like that. We never surrendered even the tenth part of what you had to give up. We didn't surrender Kiev or Minsk, let alone the Caucasus or the Volga.

RUBLYOV: Well now, you argue against yourself. Strength, then, lies in something else. You may not have surrendered Kiev or Minsk, but you fluffed the war.

VOROTYNTSEV: I can now see all this clearly, with hindsight – we didn't want to oppress our own kind; unlike you, we didn't know how. We saw no point in it. We didn't exile whole nations. We set up town councils – it is they that ruined everything for us, those liberals.

RUBLYOV: While we, even though we retreated as far as the Volga, we've conquered. We've more backbone, wouldn't you say?

VOROTYNTSEV: Yes, all those conquerors are now in your cells. If Hitler hadn't burnt their villages, they wouldn't have destroyed his Imperial Chancellery. You've had some help, from Western socialists, and from Churchill and Roosevelt in particular. Even now, in Bavaria and Austria, they've handed over excellent soldiers to you to be destroyed. What is it but blindness? It must be because to this day they haven't seen through your crimes. But the day will come when they will wake up and sort out your band of brigands properly for the first time. And this first true test will . . .

RUBLYOV (*laughing*): Never in your life, Colonel! It is *we* who will sort out their band of brigands so quickly that they will only have time to snort, the weaklings. They're as bad as Kerensky[14] in the Winter Palace!

VOROTYNTSEV: Never. This unstable world of ours will still provide pockets of courage. You have no idea how quickly weakness can turn into power, and how suddenly it can blossom in its might. We did experience this – to our own surprise.

RUBLYOV: What pockets of courage! Since you will not be leaving here, I can tell you our secret. We shall (*he approached the map, indicating*) bit by bit quietly swallow them all. They will all become part of us. Just consider your own experience. What happened to your brave rulers? Where are they now? . . . You're silent. You were all bankrupt, let me tell you. You were a generation of bankrupts. Your Ministers, your military leaders, as well as all the leaders of your political parties. Your parties themselves were bankrupt!

VOROTYNTSEV: As to the *parties*, I don't hold myself responsible.

RUBLYOV: All right, then. But you were not a small band. There were millions, or at least hundreds of thousands of you, of prosperous, well-heeled scoundrels, miserable members of the gentry, who used to irritate the people with your displays, your horse racing, your English overcoats and condescending manners. But the moment we appeared with our guns on the pavements – where did all those millions of gentlemen disappear to? Did they rush off to join General Denikin?[15] Oh no! Did they shoot at us from their attics? No, again. They joined the queues to give up their warm clothing to the Red Army. There was an order, after all, to that effect, posted up on the walls. Or else they exchanged it for lard in the market. But that's not all they did. They played cards, behind closed shutters. And they waited for the kindly, bearded Cossack with a Tsarist insignia to turn up all the way from the Don to liberate them. But who came to visit them? The Cheka. (*He laughs.*) Isn't that so? (*He roars with laughter.*) I'm talking to you like this only because you yourself fought like a man. (*A pause. He sits down.*) You won't find an answer to the puzzle of the Revolution in London. Consider – there was this prosperous mighty Empire and a handful of interlopers came along, blew on it, and the Empire was no more – things aren't as simple as that. The powerful army disintegrates. That well-intentioned, hard-working nation is led astray! With what power? With the power of our ideas!

VOROTYNTSEV: In the first place, with the power of your methods. And then, yes – with the power of your ideas.

RUBLYOV: That's just it. Go on beating your head against *that* wall.

VOROTYNTSEV: As to the power of your methods. From the very beginning your arsenal consisted of opportunist insolence and consistent cruelty. You tried to strangle your foster-brother, the Social Democrat, even while you shared the same cradle. You stole the agrarian programme from your cousin, the Social Revolutionary, bombs or no bombs. Who were you and what did you signify when you crawled out of the woodwork in the spring of 1917? The dummies of the Provisional Government could have squashed you easily and silently like a dry, anaemic bed-bug, if they hadn't been such dummies. And you would have left no trace and no smell in the annals of Russian history. But that couldn't be done! In those heady days of spring everybody had to be a European. Every opinion had a right to be heard. But you weren't going to abide by such niceties. And above all you disregarded other people's opinions. You moved by night. With your curved Tartar sabre you chopped down the cabbage heads of all those who opposed you, so that there remained but one opinion – yours!

RUBLYOV: We never concealed this. Even our banners said: 'Dictatorship'.

VOROTYNTSEV: That's just it, you didn't conceal it, while we, asses that we were, never fully understood. But how could one penetrate to the bottom of the abyss of your souls? Our Gendarmes should have taken a few lessons from your G.P.U.! Did they prosecute you in old Russia, did they fight against you? They looked after you, they nurtured you tenderly. Let's imagine a situation where some snotty boy stuck an anti-government leaflet on a fence and then got caught. According to the laws of the Russian Empire, his worst punishment would be in three months imprisonment. A Lieutenant-Colonel in the Gendarmes, fixing his pince-nez firmly on his nose, would enquire politely: 'Who are your fellow conspirators? What is your secret address? Your printing press?' 'I do not wish to answer.' 'You don't wish to answer. Fine! That's your right.' Three months later the lad comes out of prison and around his head there's a revolutionary halo, the aureole of holy martyrdom. Elderly workmen call him Mister, girls are proud to walk out on his arm, his school fellows crowd respectfully behind him. And everybody expects from him new heroic deeds, drawn from Russian literature, fully available and free. So he performs them. But look at you. Through hunger, sleeplessness and beatings you extract from him a list of fifty people who even in their dreams had never heard of the leaflet, who had never even walked along that street, but they are all seized and given ten years, while he is given twenty-five. They all go to die in Norilsk, while their surviving contemporaries remain, numb at the disappearance without trace of their friend. His sister is summoned to the Komsomol regional committee to sign her renunciation of her brother, while his father and mother, pretending to be cheerful, insist to their neighbours that their boy's gone to work in Kazakhstan. Otherwise, they will lose their flat as well as their job. Had you been treated like that, where would you be now?

RUBLYOV: To treat people like that you need a steely faith. You have always been tortured by your conscience, because you thought you had stolen something from the people.

VOROTYNTSEV: True enough. You, on the other hand, aren't tortured by it. The old Russia held twenty thousand political prisoners. They, as a matter of conscience, refused to eat their three pounds of bread, and organised university classes in their cells. Basking in the sun of Stalin's Constitution there are twenty million political prisoners. They crawl in search of herring scales in the rubbish dumps of labour camps and as to books – they might as well forget they exist. Such is the power of your methods!

RUBLYOV: Yes, I must say! We *were* tenderly nurtured ... When I was fourteen, in 1905, my father Daniel Rublyov, a railway coupler on the Moscow–Kazan line, was killed by a humane punitive detachment of your just Tsarist government.

VOROTYNTSEV: But how many were shot during that revolution? Altogether? I read somewhere that only twenty were in Kolomna.

RUBLYOV: You think that's nothing? Nothing? It was my *father* who was among them!

VOROTYNTSEV: But those were the days of the revolution, of a rebellion. While you, right across the country, when the revolution was new, shot thousands upon thousands – and in secret. That's the power of your method. Now let's talk about the power of your ideas. There was a time when your ideas had strength. They consisted of: grab what you can! You demanded nothing, you just gave away: peace, land, factories, houses. That was a convenient idea and it wasn't damaging: after all, you were distributing what didn't belong to you ...

RUBLYOV: ... created with our hands ... To that extent it belonged to us.

VOROTYNTSEV: Created with whose hands? The one who came flying in from Geneva? You awakened in millions of Russian souls the instinct of greed, of easy acquisition. And for a brief moment you were transformed from a handful into a mass movement. But before very long you had squandered Mother's inheritance and your ideas changed. Now you say: give! In other words, *they* must give everything to *you*. It's over twenty-five years since you stopped giving and started demanding. Taking: muscles, nerves, sleep, family happiness, life. So that once again, you've been transformed from a mass movement into a handful. Why is it that you're not now offering – you don't say: grab what you can?

RUBLYOV (*emerging from a bout of pain, speaking slowly*): I must admit that when I summoned you I thought you'd be talking to me . . . (*a pause*) about something else . . . (*a pause*) About that . . . (*a pause; Vorotyntsev looks fixedly at Rublyov*) migration of souls . . . about God . . .

VOROTYNTSEV: Whenever death is near, you all want to grasp at God.

RUBLYOV: That's because, probably . . . Because . . . (*he can't find the right word. Pulls himself together*): All in all, Colonel, your arguments are weak, weak! You're 69 years old, but you're as naïve as a young man. You refuse to weigh up either the overpowering might of our army or the tenacity of our centralising apparatus. You speak of handfuls and of the people. All *that* has grown together long ago like that (*he intertwines his fingers*) and it's not in human power to separate it without killing it. To shake off Bolshevism is not possible any more – you can only pull it up and half the nation with it. (*He dials a number on his telephone.*) Do you still believe in the importance of the pulse? . . . Hallo. Supper, first class, in my study.

VOROTYNTSEV: What are you talking about?

RUBLYOV: Well, a doctor – was it in Chekhov or somewhere else – a doctor arrives from town to examine a patient and he then summons the local medical assistant to a neighbouring room, for a consultation, as it were. Colleague, he says, I'm a bit worried about our patient's pulse – it's very weak. The medic, glancing at the door, says: Doctor, since we're alone, you can speak freely, you and I know that the 'pulse' doesn't exist . . . I had to put collectivisation through; I'm not boasting – I had to face a crowd with stakes, while I had no arms. I would shout loudly – you can tear me to pieces, but we'll achieve what we want! . . . But years passed and I became dimly aware that, however hard we tried, rushing from region to region, some stupid uncomprehending power emanating from Moscow was forcing us to do things in ways that were more and more painful. In 1933 they clobbered us with a wheat procurement plan on such a scale that even with the aid of the G.P.U. we could only gather forty per cent, and had to stop. Impossible to get more! Another twenty per cent, and all the peasants would have died. The President of the Inspection Committee, as well as the Secretary of the Regional Committee, wrote a report and . . . of course a month later they were both shot for being reactionary.

VOROTYNTSEV: I don't mind hearing this.

RUBLYOV: It was just at that time that an invitation came into our regional executive committee for a representative to attend a celebration of the 15th anniversary of the local Infantry Division, which was formed in our area during the Civil War. I was chosen to go. Two hotels were allocated for the guests. Carpets, ormolu. At every turn there were officers with attendants, clanking their spurs, their leather belts creaking. The doors to the banquet were flung open: 'You're invited to come in' – they nearly added: 'Officers and Gentlemen'. There were guests from Moscow, four top brass among them. Crystal glass. Silver. Exotic wines. Pastry as light as air. Silent footmen. Well, well, I thought to myself, that's after fifteen years. What will it be like after thirty?

VOROTYNTSEV: Most amusing.

RUBLYOV: After supper, there was a dance in the ballroom of the former Club of the Nobility. Invitation by ticket only, of course. Motor cars drove up to the entrance, *hoi polloi* rubber-necking, the militia dispersing the crowd. (*He sighs.*) It was then that I saw the medic was right – there is no pulse

... And the enemy, where is he? We used to think that you were the enemy. But those who sent us directives, who are they? There I sat in all the glitter, thinking of our starving little villages, who never delivered sufficient grain – I thought of Cherepinikha, of Kvasnikovka ...

VOROTYNTSEV (*gently*): Why then, after that evening, didn't you try to stand up for Kvasnikovka?

RUBLYOV: How was one to do it? Write a report to the Central Committee? That meant – to get arrested and to shoot oneself. As I said, some did and they were liquidated ... It was after that evening that I decided to flee the villages.

VOROTYNTSEV: Into the 'Organisations'.

RUBLYOV: The 'Organisations' turned up. (*A pause*): I'm no saint. My arms aren't strong enough to protect everybody.

VOROTYNTSEV: That's a pity. I too ... well, all of us, while we were in clover, argued like that and, while we argued like that, God took our souls away. You were asking about my secret. I'm going to give it to you. Stop being an executioner, lose everything and your eyes will begin to shine.

RUBLYOV: Is that all?

VOROTYNTSEV: That is all.

RUBLYOV: A bit too late to start now. And I'm not altogether convinced ...

VOROTYNTSEV: It may not be too late.

RUBLYOV: Yes, I see, you're about to start your sermon: give up your last shirt, turn the other cheek ... (*Reviving.*) Do you really think that I will concede that those who made the Revolution were rogues? You never saw those people, but I knew them personally. What right have you to call them that? The famous Muralov was the secretary of the Party Committee in the Temiryaz Academy. He was among the leaders. Ten years after the Revolution I visited him in his flat – all he had was ten square metres. The maximum allowed by the Party. And not a penny from anywhere.

VOROTYNTSEV: But the official distributors must have seen to it that he had ten times more than a worker, surely?

RUBLYOV: There was a threadbare and heavily darned table-cloth and jacket potatoes for supper. Just tell me, did your miserable Nicholas have ministers of such moral purity? At a Party discussion, Muralov spoke up for the Trostsky opposition. The regional committee instructed us to heckle, to stop him speaking. We were in the majority. But we listened to him for two hours in silence, out of sheer sympathy towards him personally, out of acute pain on his behalf. Oh dear! Did we get into trouble after that! . . . Going into exile, he took nothing with him – there was nothing to take, except a shotgun and a dog. Let me tell you something nobody else knows. I went to say goodbye to him. 'Keep your head high, Prokhor,' he told me. 'A forest doesn't weep over one tree. If people like you begin to droop – there'll be no one left. We started it, it's up to you to carry it through. Look after the Party! Take care of the Revolution!'

VOROTYNTSEV: You've achieved that all right, thanks very much! You've undermined it to an extent that no so-called reaction could have managed in twenty years. Someone once said that you need a Revolution to kill off revolutionaries.

RUBLYOV: You seem to have learnt a thing or two, now. But, earlier on, if it weren't for the Revolution, how could one have got through to the thick skulls of the ultra-reactionaries. How else could we have penetrated the minds of your Rodziankos[16] or Tereshchenkos[17] and proved to them that the time's come to give in?

A knock on the door.

WAITRESS (*in the doorway*): Permission to enter, Comrade Colonel?

Rublyov nods. A number of girls, wearing aprons, enter. The first one spreads a tablecloth and takes trays from the hands of others. There is wine. They go out silently during Vorotyntsev's speech. It is obvious that the smell of food is unpleasant for Rublyov.

VOROTYNTSEV: As far as Tereshchenko is concerned, I'm no more enamoured of the man than you are. You, with your Soviet mentality, lump together everybody who's not a Bolshevik. You could have learnt a thing or two by now. As to 'giving in' – you're quite right. The whole of world history would have been different had people learnt this one thing – how to give in from time to time. Would you like me to make a formal oration over your Revolution? Seriously. The Revolution was very useful to the whole of humanity. Those in power, the rich, are very prone to forget some things. It reminded them that an *abyss* exists. Even in the West they've grasped this. Just look how many socialisms have cropped up: Social-Fascism, National-Socialism, Social-Falangism, Radical-Socialism, Social-Catholicism – enough to get your tongue twisted. The only party in the world, don't you see, that dares to call itself conservative, is the party of Churchill. The great multitude of others elbow each other out in order to prove that they are for Progress, for Democracy, for the rights of the ordinary man. Whatever could be sweetened, has been sweetened: wherever they could give in, they did so. Who won? The French, and the Americans, the Greeks and the Italians, the Indians and the Zulus – you can cheer up – everybody won, with the exception of the Russian people. Having once shielded Europe with their flesh and blood from the Mongol whirlwind, they have done so for the second time from the hurricane of Communism. Cheer, Colonel Rublyov, why don't you cheer?

RUBLYOV: I'm quite cheerful. I'm happy, can't you see? It was I, after all, who invited you to this cheerful supper for the dying. We will uncork a bottle and drink a few carefree toasts.

VOROTYNTSEV: The horror is that you grieve over the fate of a few hundred Party dogmatists, but you care nothing about twelve million hapless peasants, ruined and exiled into the Tundra. Your conscience isn't troubled by the curses of an annihilated nation. You lose no sleep over the hatred which you have inflamed against the Russians in the Baltic provinces, on the Oder, the Visla and the Danube!

RUBLYOV: You'd have made an excellent Prosecutor! I will

drop everything and write at once to petition the Appeal
Court, Devil take it. You never know, they might even
pardon you. (*He is all contorted by pain. Eventually he straightens up.*) I would like to have seen how you would have dealt
with this cursed job, these inhuman duties, had you got as far
as my office. There's a very fine dividing line between a hero
and a prison warder. Today your eyes shine and you are
walking nobly out to your death for the sake of a lost cause,
but had history developed differently, it would have been my
eyes that would have shone and I would have called you an
executioner with some justification, while you'd have said –
fifteen days solitary. True, isn't it?

VOROTYNTSEV: You are blinded by your own myths. Our
Government never had anything approaching your Counter-Intelligence.

RUBLYOV (*pouring wine into glasses*): Well, all right. You will
have supper with me?

VOROTYNTSEV (*shying away*): Not for anything in the world!

RUBLYOV: What Asiatic barbarism! And it's you who accuse
us of Party narrow-mindedness! This duck isn't to blame,
just because it was roasted by our cook and not yours. You've
been starving for half a year. Do sit down.

VOROTYNTSEV: I wasn't starving on my own.

RUBLYOV: Well, I can't feed the lot.

VOROTYNTSEV: Such old arguments. Will you let me go
back to my cell?

RUBLYOV: Oh do sit down! (*He offers him a phial.*) Can you
read Latin?

VOROTYNTSEV (*reading*): *Venenum.* A poison. (*He returns it.*)

RUBLYOV: Death by hanging is a terrible thing! Have you
ever seen it? The hanged man is convulsed for a long time, as
if dancing, his arms separately, his legs separately, after
which each muscle, each sinew, contracts all on its own.
You're a soldier, of course. It's grist to your mill. (*He pours
the poison into both glasses.*) Let's share it. There's enough for
two. (*Vorotyntsev hesitates.*) Let's go, the pair of us. To the

other side! (*He moves the glasses nearer to himself and to Vorotyntsev. Vorotyntsev sits at the table holding his glass and is silent. Rublyov speaks very simply*): To be honest, I'm frightened to do it by myself. Frightened. While together – it's not so bad. We'll be gazing at each other as we drink. It'll burn inside for a few minutes and . . . Why drag it out? (*He attempts to clink glasses. Vorotyntsev remains silent.*) Let's clink glasses and we'll crawl under the table on all fours. Afraid as well? Or are you thinking you might get a pardon?

VOROTYNTSEV: No. I'm not thinking that.

RUBLYOV: Then, consider. Is it better to have your head put through a noose? . . . Death makes us equal. Courage! Your health, Colonel! (*He lifts his glass.*)

VOROTYNTSEV: It's a strange thing. You've caught me un-awares. I was prepared for anything, but not this . . . A pardon? No, I'm not expecting that. I know I'll be executed.

RUBLYOV: Maybe you're thinking that in a couple of days there'll be a change? That the Government will be over-turned?

VOROTYNTSEV: Alas, no! It is now entrenched for a long time. The only chance we had, the Second World War, we let slip. Now, you'll be on our backs for at least another twenty-five years. Europe is laid so low, it'll be a long time before it will rise again. It was weak towards you as far back as 1919. (*A pause.*) I don't understand it myself. Why is it that I'm prepared and yet not prepared? When I was being taken prisoner, if I'd had my gun – the English tricked me into giving it up – I could have finished it all. And I would have done so unhesitatingly. So why not now? (*He strides about the room, talking mainly to himself.*) Is there someone I haven't said goodbye to? My family? Long ago. To the inmates? Have I failed to say something that matters? That could . . . for somebody, later on . . . It looks as if being in prison brings its own new obligations. (*More loudly.*) Do you know, each extra day during which I can be of service . . . do some good . . .

Scene II

RUBLYOV (*still sitting in the same place*): There you go again, like a schoolboy. Good and Evil. Black and White. Grey-brown-purple! You can't grasp them; you can't see them. It's all twisted up and nobody can disentangle it. You're scared, eh? Why don't you admit it. It would seem, then, that I'm braver, after all.

VOROTYNTSEV (*hesitating again*): I'm ... not ... sure ...

RUBLYOV: I'm younger, you know. It's more bitter for me to die. But I don't want to go on suffering ... It would have been a good end, eh, Colonel?

VOROTYNTSEV (*looking at him, at the table, at the poison, with renewed surprise*): It's a very strange thing, ye-es. It can't be out of religious considerations: after all, I was quite prepared to shoot myself. And if death is so close ... why not a little sooner? No. I can't do it. I refuse. (*A pause.*) Perhaps it's this: you kidnapped Kutepov[18] – so what have you done with him? You've probably hanged him. And Kutepov was a friend of mine. Well, then, hang me too. Just wait, it'll be your turn for the noose soon enough.

RUBLYOV (*reaching for his telephone*): Hullo. Take him away from here into one hundred and twenty-five. (*He replaces the receiver.*) First you were in charge; then we were; a third lot will come along – and the people will remain dissatisfied and oppressed: nothing go-od will ever happen!

VOROTYNTSEV: Do you know, many years ago in Manchuria an old Chinaman predicted that I would die a soldier's death in 1945. I remembered it all this time. It helped me to be more courageous in previous wars. But as this one was coming to its end, I expected to die every day, but I lived on. The war ended. But now I'm faced with death from an enemy *after* the war. I suppose it's also a soldier's death. It's from an enemy hand. But – self-inflicted? No, that lacks dignity. That's not soldierly. That, indeed, would be cowardly. And then, why relieve you of one more murder? Why take it upon myself? No, let this, too, be your responsibility.

A guard appears in the doorway. With a wave of his hand Rublyov indicates that Vorotyntsev should be removed. Straightening himself up as an officer, his hands behind his back, Vorotyntsev leaves. Rublyov, holding his glass of poison, tries, in a croaking voice, to sing the International.

RUBLYOV: Upon us too the sun will shine.

Its brilliant warming rays . . .

Scene 12

Before the curtain rises, one can hear soft singing, in harmony, from the stage.
'Ding-dong, ding-dong, that's the clang of fetters,
Ding-dong, ding-dong, chain-gangs march and clatter . . .
The curtain rises. It is evening, the window in the cell is dark. A smoky oil lamp on a little shelf is about to go out. Mednikov is asleep by the slop bucket. Next to him, Bolosnin and Gai are talking. Further back, Mostovshchikov is telling something to a group around him, consisting of Pryanchikov and two newcomers: a Prisoner in horn-rimmed spectacles and a Prisoner with a goatee beard. To the right, downstage, Kulybyshev, Klimov and Pechkurov, sit with their legs tucked under them and sing under Rubin's direction. There is no one else in the cell.
  Rubin's choir sings:
Ding-dong, ding-dong, we march to labour camps
Ding-dong, ding-dong, we're wretched lonely tramps
They continue singing, but soundlessly.
(The rest of the scene, in the original Russian, is in verse.)

MOSTOVSHCHIKOV: Whether we fuse the light elements, or split heavy uranium, bombs will soon throw the crust of continents upwards in the form of fountains ten kilometres high. But even that does not transgress the limits, compared to what we would do if we allowed the chain reaction to escape, like a fairy-tale dragon from its cave. It will be too late, when we break through the atmosphere or crack the earth's crust. The moment we disturb the all-pervading nitrogen or upset the peaceful stillness of silicon, we shall be unable, like Goethe's sorcerer's apprentice, to contain the cataclysm.

PRYANCHIKOV (*jumping up*): No need to worry, gentlemen. There won't be time to blow up our planet. Did you know that our Sun is a 'new star'? That means that the Sun's yellow ball can explode in the twinkling of an eye and a fireball of a hundred thousand degrees will burn up both freedom in the West and the labour camps in the East!

MOSTOVSHCHIKOV: Hasn't the time come for us, scientists, to form a World Government? Can't you see how, like Hamlet and Laertes, East and West have exchanged swords? After so many centuries, humanity should not be condemned to living in hovels. But the White House will strike the Bolsheviks with the sword poisoned by the venom of the International. And the crazed, wild Soviets, summoning us back to the Dark Ages, into forests and animal skins, cling all the same to the broken edifice of Sovereignty. Thus, in a couple of decades, the culmination of centuries . . .

The hatch is being opened.

8TH SUPERVISOR: Mednikov. Without belongings!

There is a momentary silence in the cell. Mednikov shudders, lifts his head, looks around, dazed. There is a movement in the cell, an offer of help, as it were. The door is already open. Mednikov rises to his knees uncertainly. Leaning on Bolosnin and Gai, he gets up and, with his hands behind his back, moves submissively into the corridor.

Rubin's choir sings:

Ding-dong, ding-dong, that's the clang of fetters,
Ding-dong, ding-dong, chain-gangs march and clatter.

Ding-dong, ding-dong, we march to labour camps,
Ding-dong, ding-dong, we're wretched lonely tramps.

The door is shut behind Mednikov. The group at the back of the stage has broken up. Mostovshchikov and the Prisoner with a goatee beard are standing and try to walk about the cell.

MOSTOVSHCHIKOV: You wake up in the morning, sluggish from the straw, the stench, the numbness. The brain seizes up from a depressing lack of sleep. But towards the evening you get flashes of thought; your imagination is fired, you feel light, weightless, some kind of Nirvana, you know . . . It's strange.

PRISONER WITH A GOATEE BEARD: You find it strange. Not at all. The human spirit is not to be claimed by the flesh. Mahatma Gandhi fasted for ninety days! We get our rations, our prison soup, after all. We may occasionally become despondent, we may droop, and lose our faith and not know what to do, and yet our vitality, our spiritual strength, which gives us wing, is inexhaustible! I used to live full of pride and self-admiration, as if drunk with the love of life; and it is only the nocturnal shadows of prison that have revealed to me the true meaning of life . . . In freedom we are far too well fed, we are too greedy, too noisy, too quick . . . We learn the flavour of life for the first time only when we get thin prison soup and sleep on rotten straw.

BOLOSNIN (*to Gai*): We were the only ones who could have stood up in defence of a tired Europe, but in their mad ignorance they sold us – not for material gain, not for barter – but to appease Stalin's insatiable maw. The Americans sold us in Bavaria, and the English this very May hurried to betray us on the Danube. In the Russian Liberation Army there were splendid fighters, the Russian Corps, and those Cossacks after Cossacks . . . They'd seen it all in the war, they'd read all the propaganda and they'd reached the end of the line, the limit of their trust; they were ready to go anywhere – to the Devil himself, to Venus, to Caledonia, to become galley slaves – so long as it wasn't the Soviet Union!!! . . . And those Britons, who 'never, never shall be slaves' didn't overlook us. They lured our arms out of us and issued an order: all the officers are to attend a conference in Judenburg, in the English zone. I don't think that even the Ottoman Turks would have fed Christians to the dogs. Not suspecting a thing, we went trustingly, while the English left quietly by night! . . .

RUBIN (*humming to himself*): 'Night is black, night is black

[143]

Like a treacherous deed,
Like a tyrant's untrustworthy soul . . .'

PECHKUROV: What sort of song is that? Let's belt it out.

RUBIN: I don't feel up to it, friends. Tomorrow . . . Even the lamp is going out.

The lamp flickers. The scene is now dimly lit by arc lights.

KLIMOV (*patting Rubin on the shoulder*): It hurts me to listen to you, Major. You keep on saying you're a Communist – the Devil you are! You quarrel with the bastards and are quite cheerful when you are with us . . .

RUBIN: I'd rather not have such praise, Peter . . . (*He stretches out on the straw, motionless.*)

BOLOSNIN: Leafy suburbs . . . Acacia in white cascades . . . A bridge over the river. We drove up. Half-surrounded by tommy-guns. Red stars on their caps . . . Friends! We've been betrayed . . . Give us our arms! Return our arms to us! Ill-fated Russians, accursed Russian fate. Shoot oneself – there's nothing to shoot oneself with . . . It's all over . . . Pushed back as through a funnel, but they call out our names from a list . . . And someone, in his despair, jumps off the parapet onto the stones below.

The door opens with a crash. Vorotyntsev enters, holding himself very erect, very solemn.

KLIMOV: Oh Colonel!

PECHKUROV: Who did you have to see?

VOROTYNTSEV (*after a pause*): This, my sons, is our last evening. The tribunal is tomorrow. (*A pause. He embraces Klimov and Pechkurov, who have come up to him.*) Days pass and everyone's turn comes. We were close, but they will scatter us far and wide . . . A new lot will be pushed in here . . .

PRISONER WITH HORN-RIMMED SPECTACLES: A holy place is never empty.

The lamp has finally gone out. The corners of the cell are quite black. People are lit dimly.

VOROTYNTSEV: Before winter comes, where will we all be?

In which lairs to hide from freezing snowstorms? Will we be cutting up pine logs in Pechora? Or transporting the produce of the Kolyma?

BOLOSNIN (*standing up*): I will not believe that all that's left of us in this world is the dignified acceptance of hard labour in the depths of Siberian mines. Perhaps, if our great grand-father's lives ended in Siberia, their great-grandsons' will start theirs there.

VOROTYNTSEV: This belief must give you strength, yes! And, Friends, do not expect any help from the West. Prosperous countries have no will to resist, they have no strength, no conception, no understanding no . . . even when disaster stares them in the face. The hope of the world lies with you, the convicts. All of it is up to you! Maybe Russia, that has borne so much, has been waiting for people like you.

The arc lights which have been spotlighting the prisoners become gradually bronze in colour. Each prisoner, either speaking for the last time, or in silence, moves to form a group sculpture. Rubin, who is lying down leaning on one arm, and Mostovshchikov, who is leaning against the wall, are also motionless.

KULYBYSHEV: Ten years. Fifteen. Twenty-five.

PRISONER WITH A GOATEE BEARD: We're strong because we've nothing to lose.

PECHKUROV: Because, one way or another, we must all die.

GAI: But should we rebel – there's a noose. There's no turning back.

KLIMOV: There will not be an angrier soldier against Stalin.

VOROTYNTSEV: Not to have to bear the shameful disgrace . . .

BOLOSNIN: Of a labour-camp brand of slavery.

KLIMOV: Come on, snow-covered Pechora, let's feel your breath!

GAI: And you, Kolyma, straighten your shoulders!

The bronze light gradually fades. The sculptured group is motionless. Somewhere near, just beyond the window, there is the mournful howling of guard dogs, which was heard at the beginning of the play. Both the stage and the auditorium grow dark.

PECHKUROV'S VOICE: Every midnight, howling, howling of the dogs. Who are they howling for?

VOROTYNTSEV'S VOICE: 'Never send to know for whom the dogs howl; they howl for thee.'

The disjointed howling of the dogs grows ever louder.

1952–1953
Ekibastuz, Kok-Terek
during *gang-work*
orally

TRANSLATORS' NOTES

1. Supervisors were, and still are, part of the complex and oppressive Soviet system of supervision.

2. Stalin.

3. 'Decembrists' who rebelled in 1825 and were sent to Siberia.

4. Ivan Susanin: a peasant who, in 1612, saved the life of the newly elected Tsar Michael Romanov; hero of Glinka's opera *A Life for the Tsar*.

5. A reference to Pushkin's poem *The Bronze Horseman*.

6. 'The Bell': a periodical edited by Herzen and Ogaryov, in London, then in Geneva, 1857–67. 'It was the first systematic instrument of revolutionary propaganda directed against the Russian autocracy written with knowledge, sincerity and mordant eloquence.' Professor Sir Isaiah Berlin.

7. Batiy: Tatar Khan who, in 1252, subjugated South Russia and set up his 'Golden Horde'.

8. A. A. Vlasov: General in the Red Army, taken prisoner by the Germans in 1942. Agreed to head the Russian Liberation Army (c. one-million-strong). Executed as a traitor by the Russians in 1946.

9. Russian Liberation Army: set up under the aegis of the Wehrmacht, headed by General Vlasov and consisting of Soviet prisoners of war and White émigrés in the hope of liberating Russia from Bolshevik rule.

10. Taborites = Hussites.

11. Vyshinsky: (1883–1954): Foreign Minister, U.N. Delegate.

12. Beria (1899–?): Commissar for Internal Affairs, Deputy Prime Minister, disappeared after 1953 (the year of Stalin's death).

13. Stolypin, P. A. (1863–1911): Minister of Internal Affairs. Introduced agricultural reforms to help the peasantry.

14. Kerensky, A. F. (1881–1970): Member of the Fourth Duma, Premier of the Provisional Government.

15. Denikin, A. I. (1872–1947): Lieutenant General, Commander of the White Army's South-Western Front in 1917.

16. Rodzianko, M. V. (1859–1924): President of the Third and Fourth Dumas.

17. Tereshchenko, M. I. (1888–1958): Minister of Finance and Foreign Affairs in the Provisional Government.

18. Kutepov: (1882–?): Emigré White General allegedly kidnapped by the Soviets in Paris in the 'thirties.